OSCAR WILDE

Lady Windermere's Fan

With a Commentary and Notes by
PATRICIA HERN

Methuen Student Editions
METHUEN · LONDON

A METHUEN PAPERBACK

This Methuen Student Edition first published as a paperback
original in 1985 in Great Britain by Methuen London Ltd,
11 New Fetter Lane, London EC4P 4EE and in the USA by
Methuen Inc, 733 Third Avenue, New York, NY 10017.

Commentary, Chronology and Notes copyright © 1985
by Methuen London Ltd

Typeset by Words & Pictures Ltd, Thornton Heath, Surrey
Printed in Great Britain

British Library Cataloguing in Publication Data

Wilde, Oscar
   Lady Windermere's fan.— (Methuen student editions)
   I. Title   II. Hern, Patricia
   822'.8   PR5818.L2

   ISBN 0-413-57790-2

Contents

	page
Oscar Wilde: 1854-1900	v
Commentary	xii
Wilde's aesthetics	xii
Wilde's comic conventions	xvi
Lady Windermere's Fan: plot summary	xix
A 'well-made play'	xxiii
Wilde's wit	xxvii
Characters and characterisation	xxxi
Further reading	xlii
LADY WINDERMERE'S FAN	
First Act	1
Second Act	20
Third Act	56
Fourth Act	56
Notes	73

A selection of production photos appears on pp. 86-92. The upper picture on p. 88 is of the original production in 1892 (from the Raymond Mander and Joe Mitchenson Theatre Collection). All the others (by Cecil Beaton, courtesy of Sotheby's London) are from either the Haymarket in 1945 directed by John Gielgud with Isabel Jeans as Mrs Erlynne or from the Phoenix in 1966 with Coral Browne as Mrs Erlynne.

Oscar Wilde: 1854 - 1900

> I was a man who stood in symbolic relation to the art and
> culture of my age. [. . .] I made art a philosophy, and
> philosophy an art: I altered the minds of men and the colours
> of things: there was nothing I said or did that did not make
> people wonder: I took the drama, the most objective form
> known to art, and made it as personal a mode of expression as
> the lyric or the sonnet, at the same time that I widened its
> range and enriched its characterisation. [. . .] I awoke the
> imagination of my century so that it created myth and legend
> around me: I summed up all systems in a phrase, and all
> existence in an epigram. (Rupert Hart-Davis, *Selected Letters
> of Oscar Wilde*, p. 194)

Oscar Wilde made that uncompromising claim to greatness in
unlikely circumstances: he was serving a two-year prison sentence
in Reading Gaol, convicted of gross indecency, a declared bankrupt,
a man considered unfit to have custody of or even contact with his
children, pilloried in the national press, condemned by respectable
Victorian society. For many, Wilde's life illustrated the dangerous
affinity between the principles of aesthetics and the unprincipled
practices of decadence. Oscar Wilde's statement here is taken from
a long letter known as *De Profundis*, written to Lord Alfred
Douglas (1870-1945), the third son of the Marquess of Queensberry
(1844-1900), whose intimacy with Wilde led to the sensational
trials and the disgrace which ended Wilde's brilliant career as a wit,
bon viveur, poet, dramatist and aesthete in fashionable London
society. The highly publicised scandal has coloured much critical
assessment of Wilde as a writer. He himself asserted that his
life and his art were inextricably woven together as a testament to
Beauty, being deliberately organised and ornamented with more
regard for Beauty than for what Victorian society understood as
morality. He delighted in remarks such as: 'I treated Art as the
supreme reality and life as a mere mode of fiction.' (*De Profundis*,
in *Selected Letters*, p. 194.) The French writer, André Gide (1871-
1951), recalled Oscar Wilde delivering a similar epigram during a

conversation in 1895: 'Would you like to know the great drama of my life? It's that I've put my genius into my life; I've put only my talent into my work.'

1854   Born in Dublin on 16 October, a younger son of a successful
       surgeon, Sir William Wilde, and his wife, a well known Irish
       writer.

1864
-71   A boarder at Portora Royal School.

1871
-74   Read Classics at Trinity College, Dublin.

1874   February: won the Berkeley Gold Medal for Greek.

1874   A Demyship (Classics scholarship) at Magdalen College,
-78   Oxford.

1876   Travelled in Italy.

1877   Visited Ravenna and Greece.

1878   Newdigate Prize for his poem *Ravenna*.

1878   Graduated from Oxford with First Class Honours. Took a
       house in London and became an accepted part of that
       section of London society which interested itself in the
       theatre, music, painting and witty conversation.

1881   *Poems* published. They won some critical approval but little
       serious interest. 'The author possesses cleverness,
       astonishing fluency, a rich and full vocabulary, and nothing
       to say.' (*The Saturday Review*, 23 July 1881)

1882   Lecture tour of United States of America, arranged by
       Richard D'Oyly Carte (1844-1901), a theatrical impresario
       who had founded a company for the production of comic
       operas with libretti by Sir W.S. Gilbert (1836-1911) and
       music by Sir Arthur Sullivan (1842-1900). Since it was
       popularly held that Wilde had provided the model for the
       ludicrous character of Bunthorne, a 'fleshly poet' in Gilbert
       and Sullivan's opera *Patience* (1881) which D'Oyly Carte
       was taking to America, D'Oyly Carte saw Wilde's presence
       as an unusual and probably effective means of publicising
       the production, while at the same time providing a key to
       some of the opera's jokes.

1882   Wrote his first play, *Vera*. Completed *The Duchess of Padua*
       (a tragedy in the Jacobean mould) in Paris.

1884   Married Constance Lloyd.

1885   Settled in London at 16, Tite Street, Chelsea, a house
       flamboyantly adapted and decorated by the artist and

architect E.W. Godwin.

June: his first son, Cyril, born.

1886 November: his second son, Vyvyan, born.

1887 -88 Edited the journal *Woman's World* with the ambition that it should become 'the recognised organ for the expression of women's opinions on all subject of literature, art, and modern life, and yet it should be a magazine that men could read with pleasure, and consider it a privilege to contribute to'. (*Selected Letters*, p. 68)

1888 *The Happy Prince and Other Tales* published; praised for their 'charming fancies and quaint humour'. (*Athenaeum*, September 1888)

1889 Published an essay, *The Portrait of Mr. W.H.*, claiming to prove that Shakespeare had written his sonnets for a boy actor called William Hughes rather than for the Earl of Southampton.

1890 *The Picture of Dorian Gray* published. This, his only novel, created a considerable stir: many critics were shocked by the story of a beautiful young man whose portrait, hidden from public view, reflects the ravages of his life of crime and debauchery while he himself remains magically unchanged in appearance until the moment of his death. The *Daily Chronicle* of 30 June 1890 called it 'a poisonous book'.

1891 *Lord Arthur Savile's Crime and Other Stories* published, also *Intentions* in which he discussed his ideas on the nature of Art and the responsibility of the Artist. *A House of Pomegranates*, a second group of fairy stories, was published the same year. Began work on *Salomé* in Paris, writing in French. Met Lord Alfred Douglas, then a young and good-looking Oxford undergraduate attracted by Wilde's sophistication and success.

1892 *Lady Windermere's Fan* presented at the St James's Theatre, London, by the actor-manager Sir George Alexander (1858-1918). It was a popular success but won only rather grudging praise from the reviewers. 'For the staleness of the incidents one has only to refer to half a dozen familiar French plays.' (Arthur Walkley, a respected contemporary critic writing in the *Speaker*.) 'All the men talk like Mr Oscar Wilde. Everything is discussed paradoxically.' (*The Speaker*, 27 February 1892) 'The dialogue is exquisitely funny, is satirical without being aggravating to the audience. It is biting, and at the same time genial and

good-humoured.' (*Westminster Review*) This last review,
however, also dismissed the plot as 'very improbable –
impossible, one might almost add'.

1892 Began work on *A Woman of No Importance* for actor-
manager Sir Herbert Beerbohm Tree (1853-1917).

1893 February: *Salomé* published in France, but also distributed
in England. *A Woman of No Importance* produced by
Herbert Tree at the Theatre Royal, Haymarket, in London.
Critical comment was again dismissive of the plot but
appreciative of the wit.

> The story, an extremely slight one for four acts, cannot
> be regarded as pleasant or satisfactory. [. . .] The
> dialogue is brilliant, epigrammatic, paradoxical,
> antithetical even to a fault. (*The Saturday Review*)

1894 Lord Alfred Douglas's English translation of *Salomé* was
published, with illustrations by Aubrey Beardsley
(1872-98). Performance of this play was impossible in
England at that time since the Lord Chamberlain's Office
(responsible for theatre censorship) had ruled that it was
unacceptable to represent Biblical events on the stage. It
was produced in Paris by Sarah Bernhardt (1845-1923), the
leading actress of her day. *The Sphinx* published.

1895 January: *An Ideal Husband* opened at the Theatre Royal,
Haymarket. The novelist H.G. Wells (1886-1946) reviewed
it in the *Pall Mall Gazette*:

> In many ways his new production is diverting, and even
> where the fun is not of the rarest character the play
> remains interesting. And, among other things, it marks
> an interesting phase in the dramatic development of the
> author. [. . .] Oscar Wilde is, so to speak, working his
> way to innocence, as others work towards experience –
> is sloughing his epigrams slowly but surely, and
> discovering to an appreciative world, beneath the
> attenuated veil of his wit, that he, too, has a heart.

February: *The Importance of Being Earnest* was produced
with great success by George Alexander at the St James's
Theatre, London. It won praise from reviewers, such as the
critic of the London *Times*, Hamilton Fyfe, writing on this
occasion for the *New York Times*:

Oscar Wilde may be said to have at last, and by a single stroke, put his enemies under his feet. [. . .] The thing is slight in structure and as devoid of purpose as a paper balloon, but it is extraordinarily funny, and the universal assumption is that it will remain on the boards here for an indefinitely extended period.

One enemy whom Wilde conspicuously failed to put 'under his feet' was the Marquess of Queensberry, the father of Lord Alfred Douglas, who accused Wilde of alienating Douglas from his family and corrupting him. His explicit charge of gross indecency drove Wilde to sue him for criminal libel, against the advice of his friends, who feared the effect on Wilde's life and career of such a public scandal, even if he won his case. After a series of damaging testimonies against him, Wilde was compelled to withdraw his suit, then was himself arrested.

May: after two trials Wilde was found guilty of immoral and indecent conduct and sentenced to two years' imprisonment with hard labour.

November: he was transferred from Wandsworth Prison in London to Reading Gaol, where he served the rest of his sentence. It is important to understand that homosexuality was not only illegal in England at this time, but considered unspeakably decadent and corrupting by conventional Victorian society, although known to exist in bohemian or artistic circles as well as in military and naval life — there it was tolerated because remote from the centres of public activity and social behaviour. Wilde was not discreet or decorous enough to escape notoriety; he forced society to take an attitude to his relationship with Douglas, and society was outraged.

1897 In Reading Gaol he wrote a long letter to Douglas, later published under the title *De Profundis*.

1895 Wilde found the ugliness, brutality and degradation of
-97 prison life hard to endure. At first the isolation, the meagre food, the squalor and the boredom made him fear for his sanity. His suffering was aggravated by the bankruptcy proceedings against him, by his mother's death, his wife's action to establish a legal separation, and the court order forbidding him any further contact with his two sons.

I have lain in prison for nearly two years. Out of my

> nature has come wild despair; an abandonment to grief
> that was piteous to look at; terrible and impotent rage:
> bitterness and scorn: anguish that wept aloud: misery
> that could find no voice: sorrow that was dumb.
> (*Selected Letters*, p. 195)

However, before his release he appeared to have come to
terms with his situation, seeing it as a means of growing
spiritually and intellectually.

1897 May: released from prison, travelled to France, then to
Italy with Douglas. Began to work on the poem *The Ballad
of Reading Gaol* in which he tried to convey the degree of
brutilisation and isolation endured in prison, giving the
poem dramatic focus through the story of a prisoner
sentenced to death for the murder of his mistress, whose
execution disturbs the whole life of the prison and demands
some distinct moral or philosophical response from the
poet-observer. He also wrote to the newspapers on the
subject of prison reform.

1898 *The Ballad of Reading Gaol* was published, meeting with a
mixed response from the critics: some were moved by what
they felt to be its passionate authenticity; others saw it as a
spurious bid for sympathy. At least one reviewer, however,
wrote of the poem in a way which Wilde himself
acknowledged to be just and perceptive:

> We see a great spectacular intellect, to which, at last,
> pity and terror have come in their own person, and no
> longer as puppets in a play. [. . .] This poem, then, is
> partly a plea on behalf of prison reform: and, so far as
> it is written with that aim, it is not art. [. . .] For the
> poem is not really a ballad at all, but a sombre, angry,
> interrupted reverie; and it is the subcurrent of
> meditation, it is the asides, which count, not the story,
> as a story, of the drunken soldier who was hanged for
> killing a woman. (*The Saturday Review*, March 1898)

1898 December: Wilde returned to Paris.
1900 30 November: died of meningitis in Paris.
1905 *De Profundis* published.

The obituaries which appeared in the British Press reflected the
ambivalent attitude towards Wilde which has, to some extent,

survived to this day. The *Pall Mall Gazette* declared:

> Mr Wilde had wonderful cleverness, but no substantiality. His
> plays were full of bright moments, but devoid of consideration
> as drama. [. . .] He was content, for the most part, that his
> characters should sit about and talk paradoxes. [. . .] His most
> useful influence was as a corrective to British stolidity, but it
> was too diffuse to be worth much even at that.

Max Beerbohm, dramatic critic of the *Saturday Review* from 1898
to 1910, rated Wilde more highly:

> He was not a mere maker of plays. [. . .] He came as a thinker,
> a weaver of ideas, and as a wit, and as the master of literary
> style.

Some years later the critic, W.M. Leadman, writing in the
Westminster Review of August 1906, tried to see the relationship
between Wilde's life and his art in a more objective although
basically sympathetic way:

> His whole literary work (plays, poems, essays and fiction) in
> vain cried out for just criticism — prejudice, misconception, and
> a strained sense of respectability refused it. [. . .] Wilde was
> always considered a mere 'poseur'. [. . .] Great and undue stress
> was invariably laid on the man's eccentricities; in the public eye
> Wilde was only a witty fellow yearning for celebrity and capable
> of performing weird literary antics to obtain that object. He is
> indeed a tragic figure. [. . .] And yet, leaving the question of his
> conduct on one side, his sole fault was simply his unswerving
> fidelity to his own intellectual bias. He could not write about
> ordinary things in an ordinary way. [. . .] He was incapable of
> moulding his maxims on the traditional conceptions of virtue
> and vice.

Commentary

Wilde's aesthetics: the science of the beautiful

A work of art is useless as a flower is useless. A flower blossoms for its own joy. We gain a moment of joy by looking at it. (*Selected Letters*, p. 96)

The pleasure one has in creating a work of art is a purely personal pleasure, and it is for the sake of this pleasure that one creates. (To the Editor of the *Scots Observer*, July 1890: *Selected Letters*, p. 81)

Whatever I touched I made beautiful in a new mode of beauty. (*Selected Letters*, p. 194)

These statements express an attitude to art which is the basis of Wilde's 'science of the beautiful' — the phrase he used to define aesthetics for the benefit of an American journalist in 1882.

While at Oxford, between 1874 and 1878, Wilde was looking for some creed or set of principles which could give shape and expression to his own passionate appreciation of objects, experiences or ideas whose symmetry of form, or harmony and brilliance of decoration apparently separated them from common-place realities. The prosaic Victorian world of rapid industrialisation, its cities begrimed with soot and polluted by slums, was one such reality. Another was the kind of morality which seemed to mistrust pleasure, glorifying instead unsmiling toil for material gain as some guarantee of virtue, and imprisoning the imagination while encouraging hypocrisy and intolerance. This world had already been pictured and condemned by writers like Charles Dickens (1812-70) in, for example, his novels *Hard Times* (1855) and *Little Dorrit* (1857). Wilde was attracted by the English revival of Catholicism among some academics, known as the Oxford Movement and led by men such as Cardinal Newman (1801-90). In this Anglo-Catholicism (separate from Roman Catholicism) there was a renewed delight in ritual and mysticism not found in the Protestant traditions.

In March 1887 Wilde wrote to a friend:

I have a dream of a visit to Newman, of the holy sacrament in a new Church, and of a quiet and peace afterwards in my soul. I need not say, though, that I shift with every breath of thought and am weaker and more self-deceiving than ever.

If I could hope that the Church would wake in me some earnestness and purity I would go over *as a luxury*, if for no better reason. But I can hardly hope it would, and to go over to Rome would be to sacrifice and give up my two great gods, 'Money and Ambition'. (*Selected Letters*, p. 12)

He did not formally join the Roman Catholic Church until he was dying in Paris in 1900. Instead, as a young man he found that his belief in the importance of Beauty as a guiding principle could be married to his enjoyment of material comforts and social success in the service of Art. Wilde was not an innovator; his older contemporaries, John Ruskin (1819-1900), Slade Professor of Fine Art and author of many essays and articles on painting and architecture, and Walter Pater (1839-94), a Fellow of Brasenose College, Oxford, who had established himself as an authority on Aesthetics with the publication of *Studies in the History of the Renaissance* in 1873, had both already preached the doctrine of 'Art for Art's sake', representing the search for Beauty as a noble vocation, a new morality. A group of painters known as the Pre-Raphaelites were adapting the ideas of Ruskin and Pater in their exploration of a style freed from the restrictions of naturalistic perspective and familiar subjects. They drew images from Celtic as well as Classical mythology and presented them with a richness of detailed decoration which owed much to medieval church paintings and illuminated manuscripts. Shortly after leaving Oxford, Wilde spent time in Paris and London with some leaders of the Pre-Raphaelite movement, including the painter Millais (1829-96) and the painter and poet Dante Gabriel Rossetti (1828-82).

When, in May 1891, Wilde published *Intentions*, a collection of dialogues explaining his artistic principles, he emphasised the importance of Art for Art's sake rather than as a vehicle for religious or social instruction. He presented Beauty and wit rather than naturalism or work-a-day morality as the Artist's proper concerns. He now developed the idea which he had put forward in July 1890 when defending *The Picture of Dorian Gray* against accusations of decadence and obscenity; then he had written, 'An artist, sir, has no ethical sympathies at all. Virtue and weakness are to him simply what the colours on his palette are to the painter'. (*Selected Letters*, p. 81) Even later, in prison, paying a heavy price for putting his principles into practice, Wilde insisted upon the Artist's necessary freedom to seek experiences beyond the boundaries permitted by society:

> People thought it dreadful of me to have entertained at dinner the evil things of life, and to have found pleasure in their company. But they, from the point of view through which I, as an artist in life, approached them, were delightfully suggestive and stimulating. It was like feasting with panthers. (*Selected Letters*, p. 220)

Using a witty mouthpiece for his own views in the dialogue 'The Decay of Lying', Wilde rejected the Romantic reverence for Nature and the Victorians' preoccupation with the practical details of their daily routines. Nature, he asserted, was lamentably crude and unshaped, far from being the source of moral enlightenment or poetic sensibility as, for example, the poet Wordsworth (1770-1850) had claimed it to be in his Preface to the *Lyrical Ballads* and in poems such as 'Lines Written Above Tintern Abbey' or 'The Prelude'. Wilde's spokesman, Vivian, declares:

> What Art really reveals to us is Nature's lack of design, her curious crudities, her extraordinary monotony, her absolutely unfinished condition. [. . .] Art is our spirited protest, our gallant attempt to teach Nature her proper place. ('The Decay of Lying', in *Intentions*, 1891)

Vivian goes on to argue that Art takes life as its raw material to be reshaped into something entirely new, 'and keeps between herself and reality the impenetrable barrier of beautiful style, of decorative or ideal treatment'. This removal from daily life, the sense of being an artefact and therefore somehow artificial in a disturbing way, was noted and regretted by some critics who were otherwise sympathetic to Wilde's work. Even Wilde seems to have been aware of the dangers inherent in his attitude; in a letter to the writer of the Sherlock Holmes stories, Arthur Conan Doyle (1859-1930), he observed:

> Between me and life there is a mist of words always. I throw probability out of the window for the sake of a phrase, and the chance of an epigram makes me desert truth. Still, I do aim at making a work of art. (*Selected Letters*, p. 95)

He displayed contempt for 'the people', seeing the Artist as
isolated from the crowd by his genius and then persecuted for his
strangeness by those classes of society categorised by the essayist
and poet Matthew Arnold (1822-88) as Barbarians (the aristocracy)
and Philistines (the affluent middle class). As for the working class,
in one of the dialogues, 'The Critic as Artist', Wilde wrote
despairingly:

> We live in the age of the overworked, and the undereducated;
> the age in which people are so industrious that they become
> absolutely stupid. [. . .] Those who try to lead the people can
> only do so by following the mob.

Later in the same dialogue the leading character remarks: 'Yes, the
public is wonderfully tolerant. It forgives everything except genius.'
These sentiments make Wilde's choice of the theatre as a vehicle
for *his* genius seem like an act of defiance. Certainly his cynicism
about Victorian England is reflected in his portrayal of a society
peopled largely by dilettantes, charlatans and privileged fools. Even
his heroes, like Lord Goring in *An Ideal Husband*, affect an air of
frivolous conceit to hide their true worth. In *The Importance of
Being Earnest* Lady Brackness says: 'Never speak disrespectfully of
Society, Algernon. Only people who can't get into it do that'. (p. 63)
Wilde's attitude was ambivalent: on the one hand, he enjoyed his
personal success in the fashionable world of London's salons,
restaurants and theatres, using the wealth and the way of life he
found there both to inspire and to set off his own wit; on the other
hand, he was evidently aware of its complacency, its artificiality, its
hypocrisy, its cruelty towards those it felt threatened by or could
not place comfortably. He drew on his knowledge of Society and,
to a large extent, depended on his audience's recognition of the
manners and the social taboos governing the characters' actions.
This direct reference to the real world in his own plays may seem
inconsistent in one who condemned contemporary English
melodrama because: 'The characters in these plays talk on the
stage exactly as they would talk off it; they have neither
aspirations nor aspirates; they are taken directly from life and
reproduce its vulgarity down to the smallest detail.' ('The Decay of
Lying', in *Intentions*, 1891) However, Wilde's plays do not simply
hold up a mirror to nature, rather they present an elaborate and
stylised vision, or revision, of carefully selected images. A
contemporary critic and dramatist, St. John Hankin, remarked that
Wilde presented only 'brilliant surface', never the soul of the character.

This was a deliberate decision by Wilde, not an artistic failure; in
'The Decay of Lying' the protagonist, Vivian, sees the nineteenth
century's struggle to reveal human nature in Art as leading only to
boring uniformity, since what distinguishes one man from his
neighbour are external features such as dress, manners, appearance
and voiced opinions — man discovered through his behaviour in
company, not through solitary soul-searchings or communion with
Nature. At the end of the dialogue Vivian sums up the guiding
principles of 'the new aesthetics':

> Briefly, then, they are these. Art never expresses anything but
> itself. It has an independent life. [. . .] It is not necessarily
> realistic in an age of realism, nor spiritual in an age of faith. [. . .]
>
> The second doctrine is this. All bad art comes from returning
> to Life and Nature, and elevating them into ideals. [. . .] As a
> method Realism is a complete failure. [. . .]
>
> The third doctrine is that Life imitates Art far more than Art
> imitates Life. This results not merely from Life's imitative
> instinct, but from the fact that the self-conscious aim of Life
> is to find expression, and that Art offers it certain beautiful
> forms through which it may realise that energy. [. . .]
>
> The final revelation is that Lying, the telling of beautiful
> untrue things, is the proper aim of Art. (*Intentions* 1891)

Wilde's comic conventions

Wilde's concern with 'brilliant surface' placed him within a
recognisable English tradition. In presenting Society to Society,
with its heroes as those who were most accomplished, most elegant
and most successful in the 'beau monde', and by mocking interlopers
from the vulgar world of commerce or the colonies, Wilde revived the
spirit of the late seventeenth-century Restoration Comedy, the style
of Congreve (1670-1729) and Wycherley (1640-1716). Congreve's
comic scenes, for instance, depend upon the audience's acceptance
of an etiquette governing all aspects of social life, so that a gaffe
was recognisable and laughable. The wit was polished, sophisticated
and elitist. It worked through highly structured word-play rather
than slapstick or clowning. His characters display a real or affected
cynicism, speaking of marriage as an indispensable but often
intolerable condition of life in a society that values wealth and status
more than virtue and good nature. For example, in *The Way of the
World* (1700) Mistress Fainall and Mistress Marwood discuss the
prospect of marriage in a way that Wilde's Duchess of Berwick and

Lady Plymdale would perfectly have understood:

> MRS. FAINALL. Is it possible? Dost thou hate those Vipers Men?
> MRS. MARWOOD. I have done hating 'em, and am now come to
> despise 'em; the next thing I have to do, is eternally to
> forget 'em.
> MRS. FAINALL. There spoke the Spirit of an Amazon, a
> Penthesilea.
> MRS. MARWOOD. And yet I am thinking sometimes to carry my
> Aversion further.
> MRS. FAINALL. How?
> MRS. MARWOOD. Faith by marrying; if I could but find one
> that lov'd me very well, and would be thoroughly sensible
> of ill Usage, I think I should do myself the Violence of
> undergoing the Ceremony.

Congreve's London is inhabited by pleasure-seeking young men,
competing with each other to reduce life, love and lust to neatly
turned epigrams, just as Dumby and Cecil Graham do; *The Way of
the World* starts in this way as the hero, Mirabell, expresses
indifference over his defeat at cards by his friend Fainall:

> FAINALL. . . . . the Coldness of a losing Gamester lessens the
> Pleasure of the Winner. I'd no more play with a Man that
> slighted his ill Fortune, that I'd make Love to a Woman who
> undervalu'd the Loss of her Reputation.

Although Wilde's characters can display the kind of stylised and
therefore perhaps rather brittle-seeming brilliance of the earlier
Restoration wits, what might be called his 'problem plays' – such
as *Lady Windermere's Fan* and *An Ideal Husband* – have an
underlying warmth of feeling and a concern for the unhappiness
found inside Society's elegant houses, which hark back to the more
humane comedies of Farquhar (1677-1707). In Farquhar's *The Beaux'
Stratagem* (1707), for instance, young Aimwell finds himself changed
by love, just as Lord Darlington is, and is startled into virtue himself
by the example of the woman he loves

> AIMWELL (*aside*). Such goodness who could injure! I find myself
> unequal to the task of villain; she has gained my soul, and
> made it honest like her own. I cannot, cannot hurt her.
> (Act V, scene iv)

Farquhar allows one of his characters seriously to question the

degree of unhappiness that must be endured before the marriage
bond can justifiably be broken by one of the partners. Mrs Sullen
is married to a man she loathes, whom she finds physically
distasteful and who treats her with little affection and no respect.
She feels imprisoned within the institution:

> MRS. SULLEN. Were I born a humble Turk, where women
>   have no soul nor property, there I must sit contented.
>   But in England, a country whose women are its glory, must
>   women be abused? Where women rule, must women be
>   enslaved? Nay, cheated into slavery, mocked by a promise
>   of comfortable society into a wilderness of solitude! I dare
>   not keep the thought about me. (Act IV, scene i)

Wilde allows Lord Darlington to question the justice of a moral code
which requires a woman to endure passively the infidelity of her
husband (p. 31): 'It's wrong for a wife to remain with a man who
so dishonours her'. In each case the dramatist finds a solution that
will bring his play to the 'happy ending' expected of a comedy:
Farquhar more adventurously offers mutually agreed divorce to his
lady and her husband; Wilde dispels Lady Windermere's distress so
as to keep her happily within the marriage, thus reinforcing rather
than challenging his society's conventions.

Just as the small theatres of the Restoration period catered for
an exclusive, privileged and leisured class, so the audiences at the
St James's Theatre or the Theatre Royal, Haymarket, in the 1890s
were predominantly either rich and aristocratic or fashionably
bohemian. The 1860s and 1870s had seen a change in London's
theatrical life: crude farces, bawdy burlesques and sensational
melodramas no longer dominated the stages of the fashionable West
End. Under the influence of actor-managers like Sir Herbert Tree,
George Alexander and Sir Henry Irving and of playwrights such as
Tom Robertson, polite society no longer had to rely upon the Opera
for acceptable – or respectable – entertainment. With a series of
plays, including *Society* (1865) and *Caste* (1867), produced at the
Prince of Wales's Theatre in London, Robertson inaugurated what
has been called 'the cup-and-saucer drama', since it dealt with
realistic, contemporary and domestic life. Wilde referred scornfully
to the characters: 'they present the gait, manner, costume and accent
of real people; they would pass unnoticed in a third-class railway
carriage' ('The Decay of Lying'). Yet he benefited from the
creation of a new and influential audience, so that the wife of

George Alexander — the actor-manager who first staged *Lady Windermere's Fan* — could write delightedly:

> Our first nights at the St. James's Theatre were like brilliant parties. Everybody knew everybody, everybody put on their best clothes, everybody wished us success. (Cited by A.E.W. Mason in *Sir George Alexander at the St. James's Theatre.*)

Wilde's characters are defined by their social status and revealed through their manners in a way, therefore, that perfectly complemented the interests and experiences of his patrons. They belong to recognisable groups: the witty young man-about-town in search of amusement and, eventually, a rich and respectable wife; the daunting dowager or formidable mother of such an eligible would-be bride; the glamorous and often dangerous woman-of-the-world, full of biting wit and sophistication but — because of the worldliness and wickedness which make her attractive — only to be flirted with and not welcomed into the family; the ingénue, a sweet young girl, occasionally precocious in manner but always uncorrupted by experience, and preferably with a large dowry and prestigious relatives to maker her even more attractive. These required the presence of a servant class equally governed by etiquette and nice distinctions of rank, like the Windermeres' imperturbable butler, Parker.

Lady Windermere's Fan: plot summary

Act I

It is the afternoon of Lady Windermere's twenty-first birthday; she has, according to custom, 'come of age', that is, reached maturity. She is at home, arranging flowers in readiness for her celebration dance and dinner that evening. Lord Darlington, a wealthy and fashionable friend of Lord Windermere, who greatly admires Lady Windermere, calls on her. He admires the fan which her husband has given her as a birthday present, is flirtatious — to her annoyance — then more earnestly offers her his friendship should she ever need it. He suggests that any wife whose husband is unfaithful to her should feel free to take a lover herself. Lady Windermere is deeply shocked and certainly sees no connection with her own situation.

The Duchess of Berwick arrives, trailing her submissive, marriageable daughter with her. She has come to tell Lady Windermere that her husband is, it seems, having an affair with a sophisticated, fascinating middle-aged woman called Mrs. Erlynne. Mrs. Erlynne is regarded with suspicion by polite society who believe her to have at least one scandal in her past. Lord Windermere has been seen visiting her regularly and is thought to be giving her large sums of money which enable her to live stylishly in the most fashionable part of London. Lady Windermere will not believe ill of her husband; they married for love only two years earlier and have a six-month-old child. However, when alone, she examines her husband's account books and is appalled to discover the record of repeated and substantial payments to Mrs. Erlynne. Lord Windermere is angry to find her looking at his private documents and protests his innocence when she accuses him of being Mrs. Erlynne's lover. He explains that Mrs. Erlynne foolishly gave up her place in respectable society and abandoned her marriage when she was much the same age as Lady Windermere, but has since suffered in exile and now wishes to re-enter society. To do so she needs the support of someone as respectable and respected as Lady Windermere. He asks his wife to receive Mrs. Erlynne at their party that evening but she threatens to strike Mrs. Erlynne across the face with her new fan should the woman enter the Windermeres' house. Left alone, Lord Windermere sinks down in despair, distraught that he dare not tell his wife the truth about Mrs. Erlynne's identity. He does not explain these words.

Act II

That evening Lady Windermere is welcoming her guests, including the Duchess of Berwick and the wealthy young Australian to whom the Duchess wishes to marry her daughter, Agatha. The Duchess's brother, Lord Augustus Lorton — known as Tuppy to his friends — consults Lord Windermere about how to deal with Mrs. Erlynne. Lord Augustus, a foolish but good-natured man, is fascinated and charmed by Mrs. Erlynne but needs reassurance that she would be acceptable as his wife. He is pleased to learn that Mrs. Erlynne is to be a guest at Lady Windermere's party. Lady Windermere confides in Lord Darlington that she is, indeed, in need of a friend. He offers her love rather than friendship, urging her to leave her apparently unfaithful husband and elope with him to Europe where they will eventually marry. Lady Windermere shrinks from the idea. When Mrs. Erlynne arrives Lady Windermere lacks the resolution to strike her with the fan. Later Lady Windermere overhears Mrs. Erlynne

asking Lord Windermere for a large sum of money to make her
hoped-for marriage to Lord Augustus more acceptable in his eyes
and the eyes of his family and friends. Shocked by Mrs. Erlynne's
evident hold over Lord Windermere, Lady Windermere decides to
go away with Lord Darlington in spite of the disgrace this will bring
upon her. She writes her husband a letter explaining her decision,
then leaves. Mrs. Erlynne discovers the letter and is appalled to
think that Lady Windermere — who is in fact the daughter she
abandoned twenty years before — might repeat her own ruinous
action and leave her husband and child. She decides to save her
daughter from remorse and shame, so takes the letter and follows
Lady Windermere, leaving a message that Lady Windermere has
retired to bed with a headache, and instructing Lord Augustus to
keep Lord Windermere away from home all night if possible.

Act III
Later that night in Lord Darlington's appartment, Lady Windermere
is waiting, alone. She hopes that her husband will come to protest
his love and take her back home. She regrets her impulsive action
but feels that she cannot herself reverse the decision she has so
rashly made. Yet, when Mrs. Erlynne arrives, Lady Windermere at
first resists her impassioned persuasion to return home before her
absence is noticed. However, when Mrs. Erlynne speaks of her duty
to her child, Lady Windermere's resistance breaks and she begs for
help. At that moment they hear the voices of Lord Darlington and
his friends. Knowing that it would bring dishonour on a woman
to be found so late at night in a bachelor's rooms, Mrs. Erlynne
tells Lady Windermere to hide behind a curtain and escape when
possible. She herself is particularly disturbed to hear the voice of
Lord Augustus as her discovery here would destroy her hopes of
marriage to him. She retreats into the next room. Lord Windermere
is also present, unaware of the significance of Lord Darlington's
references to the good woman he loves who will not leave her
husband despite her unhappiness. One of the men present is amused
to find a lady's fan in Lord Darlington's apartment. He shows it to
Lord Windermere, who is shocked to recognise it as the one he gave
his wife for her birthday. Lord Windermere demands the right to
search Lord Darlington's rooms but is forestalled by Mrs. Erlynne's
appearance from the next room. She claims to have taken the fan
by mistake when leaving the Windermeres' house earlier. In the
confusion, Lady Windermere makes her escape, unnoticed.

Act IV

The following morning Lady Windermere is at home, distressed and
afraid Mrs. Erlynne will have told Lord Windermere the truth to
protect her own interests. However, when her husband appears he
is simply concerned for her well-being. His contempt for Mrs. Erlynne
and regret at having forced her presence upon his wife the previous
evening make it plain that Lady Windermere's secret is still safe. He is
reluctant for his wife to receive Mrs. Erlynne again when she calls
to return the fan, but Lady Windermere is desperate to show her
gratitude to Mrs. Erlynne for rescuing her from shame and ruin
and for sacrificing her own reputation in order to preserve Lady
Windermere's. Mrs. Erlynne asks for a picture of Lady Windermere
and her child as a memento. Alone briefly with Lord Windermere,
Mrs. Erlynne listens to his condemnation of her dishonesty and lack
of honour. She makes no attempt to excuse her presence in Lord
Darlington's apartment but comments with bitter irony on her new
relationship with her daughter: she has been hurt and hindered in
her ambitions by the sudden and unexpected power of her maternal
feelings, so intends to separate her life from her daughter's again
without revealing her true identity. Lord Windermere does not
understand the real significance of her comments, seeing them merely
as cynical and selfish. Lady Windermere returns with the photograph.
She has a few moments alone with Mrs. Erlynne when she tries to
thank her and promises to confess everything to her husband, but
Mrs. Erlynne urges her to remain silent rather than risk destroying
her husband's love and, at the same time, making pointless
Mrs. Erlynne's one unselfish action. Mrs. Erlynne asks for the fan
as a keepsake. Lord Augustus arrives and is shocked to see
Mrs. Erlynne who he feels has betrayed him. She persuades him to
escort her to her carriage and when he returns it is with jubilation —
he has accepted her story that she had gone to Lord Darlington's
rooms innocently in her anxiety to tell Lord Augustus as soon as
possible that she would consent to marry him, but had been
terrified by the arrival of so many men and therefore hidden. What
had seemed shameless now seems courageous.

  Thus the play ends happily, with Lady Windermere having truly
'come of age' now that she has shed her immature intolerance and
self-righteousness without damaging her relationship with her
husband, and with Mrs. Erlynne's 'good deed' rewarded by marriage
to Lord Augustus.

A 'well-made play'

Contemporary reviewers of Wilde's plays commented slightingly on his use of stereotyped or absurdly contrived plot-lines as mere vehicles for his wit. When *Lady Windermere's Fan* was revived in 1904, four years after Wilde's death, the essayist, critic and wit, Max Beerbohm, combined a critique of the play with a more general assessment of Wilde's qualities as a dramatist:

> He did not at first take the theatre seriously. He was content to express himself through the handiest current form of play. And that form happened to be Sardouesque comedy. It is inevitable, therefore, that *Lady Windermere's Fan* should seem to us now, after the lapse of twelve years [since its first production], old-fashioned in its scheme. But it is old-fashioned only in the sense in which a classic is old-fashioned. Partly by reason of the skill with which the scheme is treated [. . .] and much more by reason of the dialogue itself, which is incomparable in the musical elegance and swiftness of its wit, *Lady Windermere's Fan* is a classic assuredly. (*Last Theatres 1904-1910*, Max Beerbohm, Rupert Hart-Davis, London 1970, p. 102)

Beerbohm's reference to 'the handiest current form of play' arose from the fashion then for what have since been called 'well-made plays'. These came into the English repertory as adaptations of comedies by French dramatists such as Scribe (1791-1861) and Sardou (1831-1908). Scribe's principle of construction was to arrange key events and sensations so that the audience should be kept expectant and intrigued from beginning to end — then a play was 'well made'. Sardou's formula was more precise; his plays have a brisk exposition in which the main characters and their situation are introduced as quickly as possible, then there comes a series of misunderstandings or confusions, often linked to a particular object such as a letter or a fan, with coincidence used to move the plot forward to the final resolution should character or situation prove inadequate motivation. Suspense was generated and maintained by the audience's knowledge that a skeleton from the leading character's past or a guilty secret in their present would certainly disrupt the surface calm.

Lady Windermere's Fan is in four acts. Act One introduces the world of London's polite Society during the Season, that period from May to July when the rich, the aristocratic and the fashionable went through a routine of receptions and balls, and when ambitious

mothers competed to secure wealthy and well-connected husbands
for their daughters of marriageable age. The Windermeres are placed
at the centre of the action and quickly linked to the two 'problem'
characters, Lord Darlington and Mrs. Erlynne. The characteristics
of each are described or demonstrated: Lady Windermere's youthful
complacency and earnest, ungenerous morality; Lord Darlington's
witty affectation of idle, frivolous decadence, interrupted to reveal
his serious feelings; Lord Windermere's passion and forcefulness;
Mrs. Erlynne's sophistication and scent of scandal. The play's central
preoccupations are also discussed: the rightness or wrongness of
society's division of people into 'good and bad', acceptable and
inadmissible, and of transgressions into forgivable 'little aberrations'
or unforgivable moral crimes. At the end of the act the apparent
tranquillity of the Windermere world is disrupted by stories of
Mrs. Erlynne's invasion of fasionable London and by Lady
Windermere's sudden belief in her husband's infidelity. True to the
spirit of Scribe and Sardou, Wilde leads the audience's interest
on to the next act with Lord Windermere's teasing reference to
Mrs. Erlynne and his wife. He poses a question for the audience to
consider during the first interval (p. 19):

> LORD WINDERMERE. My God! What shall I do? I dare not tell
>   her who this woman really is. The shame would kill her.
>   (*Sinks down into a chair and buries his face in his hands.*)

Clearly someone will be required to do something, the situation
cannot remain static, and so the movement of the plot begins to
create a momentum which will carry it to the final resolution and
the re-establishment of tranquillity and rest.

In Act Two the suspense already generated by Lady Windermere's
threat to strike Mrs. Erlynne with her new fan sustains the audience's
expectancy through Wilde's mocking representation of social
conversation. The plot possibilities offered by Mrs. Erlynne are
extended by Lord Augustus's willingness to marry her if she can be
assured of the approval of Society as represented by the Windermeres.
That 'if' creates effective tension in the next two acts. By the end
of Act Two disaster has been precipitated by Lady Windermere's
reckless decision to elope with Lord Darlington and the possibility
of rescue promised by Mrs. Erlynne's pursuit of her.

Act Three exploits a situation also used by Wilde in Act Three of
An Ideal Husband; the reception room of a bachelor's apartment,
a door behind which a woman retreats to hide, her reputation in peril,

and added tension created by misunderstandings over her identity
once her presence has been betrayed. It is a stratagem common in
farce also, but here the tension is not comic, for Wilde could rely
on his audience's appreciation of the seriousness of the woman's
predicament and the reality of the husband's sense of outrage that
that woman might be his wife. The act begins strongly with the
pathos and anguish of Lady Windermere's plight and her hopeless
longing for her husband to rescue her from the consequences of
her rash flight from home, followed by the passionate conflict and
poignant reconciliation between her and the woman the audience
know to be her mother. Just as the danger appears to fade, it is most
vigorously renewed by the arrival of the men, trapping the two
women in a conspiracy of terror. The audience, too, are necessarily
part of the conspiracy, unable to betray the women yet unable to
help them. Once again Wilde follows a crisis with an interlude of
witty exchanges, an opportunity to display his virtuosity with
epigram and paradox. Just as the mood seems to lighten, the
discovery of Lady Windermere's fan dramatically revives the suspense
and the audience wait to witness the women's disgrace or their
miraculous delivery. Lord Windermere rushes towards his wife's
hiding place – the catastrophe seems inevitable – but Mrs. Erlynne's
sudden appearance at the last moment transforms the event and
creates a new climax, giving further food for speculation during the
next interval. Like Lady Windermere, the audience must want to
know what happens after her escape from 'that horrible room'.

Lady Windermere's brief soliloquy at the beginning of Act Four
recalls the anguish of the previous act, so that the momentum of the
plot is not lost. The entry of Lord Windermere into his own
morning-room becomes charged with tension because of what the
audience – and Lady Windermere – do not know and what they
imagine *might* be his state of mind. Wilde works towards the
resolution by creating small crises which he then deftly dissolves,
while at the same time striving for symmetry and balance in the play
by referring back to conflicts and confusions from Act One. Lady
Windermere is about to confess all – suspense – but is prevented by
the announcement of Mrs. Erlynne's arrival. She is bringing back
the fan with which she was to have been struck the previous day.
The disagreement as to whether she should or should not be received
by Lady Windermere – so bitterly argued in Act One – is renewed,
but the positions are reversed. Lady Windermere is shown to have
learnt about temptation and remorse; she has acquired a kind of

enlightenment whereas her husband has regressed to the harshness
of his society's moral conventions. Mrs. Erlynne is admitted on the
strength of a shared secret — as she was earlier. The question posed
at the end of Act One (who is Mrs. Erlynne and what is the nature
of her hold over Lord Windermere?) is fully answered and her future
settled — still a life of exile, but given the comfort and respectability
of marriage to Lord Augustus. At the end of the play all the plot-lines
are neatly tied up, but this does not simply re-establish the former
status quo: Lady Windermere has herself become a 'woman with a
past'. It is well that Mrs. Erlynne burned the letter Lady Windermere
wrote announcing her plan to elope with Lord Darlington, otherwise
it might have provided the basis for another well-made play in which
Lady Windermere's middle-aged serenity was threatened by the
possible exposure of her youthful folly.

Wilde's original idea of the play differed significantly from the
final version. During rehearsals, George Alexander (actor-manager
of the St. James's Theatre) urged Wilde to change his first scheme
to delay the revelation of Mrs. Erlynne's true identity. There was a
conflict between maintaining the uncertainty for as long as possible
and exploiting the possibilities for more interesting character-
development and dramatic irony which lay in the audience's
knowledge of the truth — especially while Lady Windermere
remained in ignorance. Originally Wilde delayed the revelation until
Act Four. In a letter to Alexander he defended this decision:

> With regard to your other suggestion about the disclosure of the
> secret of the play in the second act, had I intended to let out the
> secret, which is the element of surprise and curiosity, a quality
> so essentially dramatic, I would have written the play on entirely
> different lines. I would have made Mrs. Erlynne a vulgar horrid
> woman and struck out the incident of the fan. The audience
> must not know till the last act that the woman Lady Windermere
> proposed to strike with her fan was her own mother. The note
> would be too harsh, too horrible. When they learn it, it is after
> Lady Windermere has left her husband's house to seek the
> protection of another man, and their interest is concentrated on
> Mrs. Erlynne, to whom dramatically speaking belongs the last
> act. Also it would destroy the dramatic wonder excited by the
> incident of Mrs. Erlynne taking the letter and opening it and
> sacrificing herself in the third act. If they knew Mrs. Erlynne
> was the mother, there would be no surprise in her sacrifice — it

would be expected. [. . .] Also it would destroy the last act: and
the chief merit of my last act is to me the fact that it does not
contain, as most plays do, the explanation of what the audience
knows already, but that it is the sudden explanation of what the
audience desires to know, followed immediately by the revelation
of a character as yet untouched by literature. (*The Letters of
Oscar Wilde*, edited by Rubert Hart-Davis, pp. 308-309)

However, Wilde was persuaded to recognise the stronger claims of
the psychological needs of his characters and to give the audience
the information necessary for a sympathetic understanding of
Mrs. Erlynne's predicament. In a letter to the editor of the *St. James's
Gazette* he explained that his change of heart was occasioned by the
response of his friends to the play's first performance, then still in
its original form:

> The opinions of the old on matters of Art are, of course, of no
> value whatsoever. The artistic instincts of the young are
> invariably fascinating; and I am bound to state that all of my
> friends, without exception, were of opinion that the psychological
> interest of the second act would be greatly increased by the
> disclosure of the actual relationship existing between Lady
> Windermere and Mrs. Erlynne — an opinion, I may add, that
> had previously been strongly held and urged by Mr. Alexander.
> As to those of us who do not look on a play as a mere question
> of pantomime and clowning, psychological interest is everything,
> I determined consequently to make a change in the precise
> moment of revelation (*Letters of Oscar Wilde*, p. 313).

Alexander's other alteration, accepted by Wilde, was to lighten
the end of Act Two; instead of allowing Mrs. Erlynne to rush off
with barely a word to the bewildered Lord Augustus, Alexander
had provided her with an additional speech which Wilde described
as 'adequate' while protesting that he should have been consulted
before his play was tampered with. Wilde then reshaped the ending
of the act, giving Lord Augustus the final, wry word: 'Well, really,
I might be her husband already. Positively I might'. (p. 39)

Wilde's wit: the art of paradox and epigram

From the first reviews of his early poetry, through to the obituaries
which attempted to evaluate his life's work, emphasis was placed
on the beauty and wit of Wilde's style. H.G. Wells, writing in the

xxviii LADY WINDERMERE'S FAN

Daily News in October 1909, argued that behind the apparent
evenness of style there lay a significant variation in quality:

> Wilde knew how to say the precise thing which, whether true or
> false, is irresistible. [. . .] One might go through his swift and
> sparkling plays with a red and blue pencil marking two kinds of
> epigrams; the real epigram which he wrote to please his own
> wild intellect, and the sham epigram he wrote to thrill the very
> tamest part of our tame civilisation. [. . .] He lowered himself
> to superiority; he stooped to conquer.

An *epigram* is a balanced statement encapsulating a clever or comic
thought. It involves reducing a moral system or a social attitude
to a neatly turned phrase. The wit, in the eighteenth-century sense
of a creative, cultivated intelligence, is conspicuous. There are many
examples of epigram in *Lady Windermere's Fan*, distributed among
several of the characters.

> CECIL GRAHAM. Wicked women bother one. Good women
>   bore one. That is the only difference between them. (p. 27)
> DUMBY. Experience is the name everyone gives to their mistakes.
>   (p. 53)
> DUCHESS OF BERWICK. Men become old, but they never
>   become good. (p. 12)

These not only have a satisfying and persuasive rhythm and symmetry
in their form, but can also contain a variety of attitudes or values
within one statement. For example, Cecil Graham remarks (p. 51):

> Well, there's nothing in the world like the devotion of a married
> woman. It's a thing no married man knows anything about.

Graham's comment can mean that married men (husbands) are
incapable of recognising the devotion shown to them by their wives
because they themselves are too frivolous and faithless; however, it
can also mean that married women direct their devotion, not towards
their husbands, but always towards the still unmarried men of their
acquaintance. It is the irony implicit in this ambiguity that gives
the remark its wit. Wilde's epigrams sometimes made their effect
by putting neatly into words what many people already knew or
believed. For instance:

> MRS. ERLYNNE. He thinks like a Tory and talks like a Radical,
> and that's so important nowadays. (p. 27)

> DUCHESS OF BERWICK. Love — well, not love at first sight
> but love at the end of the season, which is so much more
> satisfactory. (p. 34)

Wilde's *paradoxes* represent a specific style of epigram — that is, the
association within one statement of two apparently contradictory
ideas in order to challenge accepted conventions or to suggest new
ones. Here, too, part of the humour lies in a recognition of the
cliché or the convention supporting the paradox. As the Victorian
critic, Ernest Newman, argued in *Free Review* (1.6.1895):

> The function of paradox is to illuminate light places, to explain
> just those things that everybody understands. [. . .] To hear one
> of Mr. Wilde's paradoxes by itself is to be startled; to read them
> in their proper context is to recognise the great fact on which
> I have already insisted, that a paradox is a truth seen round
> a corner.

The audience may laugh because the expectations set up in the first
part of the statement are overturned by the incongruous or
unconventional nature of the second part. When, for example,
Lord Darlington declares (p. 6): 'I can resist everything . . .', one
might expect him to qualify that by naming one or two particular
weaknesses in his otherwise admirable life of self-denial. However,
his qualifying comment comically cancels out the moral stance
implicit in the first part: '. . . except temptation.' Other paradoxes
more clearly support Ernest Newman's emphasis on the importance
of their particular context; it is, for example, important to remember
Mrs. Erlynne's character and situation in order to appreciate Dumby's
remark (p. 49): 'Mrs. Erlynne has a past before her.'
   The humour of paradox and epigram requires an appreciation
not only of language's ability to convey truths or to challenge
attitudes, but also of the way in which language itself can become
absurdly conventional and affected. There is, for instance, the
commonplace greeting: 'How do you do?' or 'How are you?'; its use
is merely formal, it is a greeting rather than a genuine inquiry into
the health of an acquaintance. Wilde allows Cecil Graham to underline
the possible absurdity of such formalities (p. 24):

> CECIL GRAHAM. Good evening, Arthur. Why don't you ask me
> how I am? I like people to ask me how I am. It shows a
> wide-spread interest in my health.

Sometimes Wilde takes a familiar idiom or figure of speech and adapts it for comic effect. For example, in Act Three Dumby follows Cecil Graham's teasing of Lord Augustus with the comment (p. 49):

> The youth of the present day are quite monstrous. They have absolutely no respect for dyed hair.

The humour lies in one's recognising the corruption of the more usual complaint that young people do not treat their *white-haired* elders and betters with more respect. Wilde is also mocking the vanity of those who dye their hair in order to appear younger than they are, as well as reflecting the kind of affectation fashionable in his society and represented here by Dumby. Wilde delighted in the attention paid by his fashionable contemporaries to elegance of phrase and sparkling repartee, while at the same time recognising the shallowness and artificiality that such a concern for polish and poise could produce. Lord Darlington — whose elegant frivolousness is shown to be only a decorative cover for his deeper passions — passes judgment on Cecil Graham (p. 24): 'You're excessively trivial, my dear boy, excessively trivial!' Nonetheless, Wilde took advantage of the opportunities for epigram and repartee offered by otherwise rather flat or two-dimensional characters like Dumby and Cecil Graham. Even Lord Darlington, suffering from the rejection of his proposal to Lady Windermere, can play his part in a kind of social game in which one player makes an opening gambit — asks a question or makes a challenging statement — to allow the next player to score a point by providing a witty answer or by deflecting the possible hostility of the first comment. Lord Windermere is annoyed by the suggestive remarks Graham and Dumby are making about Mrs. Erlynne (p. 50):

> LORD WINDERMERE. Dumby, you are ridiculous, and Cecil, you let your tongue run away with you. You must leave Mrs. Erlynne alone. You don't really know anything about her, and you're always talking scandal against her.

Cecil Graham is undismayed and takes the sting out of the criticism by amending Lord Windermere's choice of words:

> GRAHAM. My dear Arthur, I never talk scandal. *I* only talk gossip.

Irritable though he may be, Lord Windermere is made to play the game by asking the question which allows Graham to finish the round with a couple of polished epigrams:

> GRAHAM: Oh! gossip is charming! History is merely gossip. But scandal is gossip made tedious by morality.

A little later in the same scene, Wilde shows how conversation can become competitive, with each participant trying to better the wit of the man before (p. 52):

> LORD DARLINGTON. What cynics you fellows are!
> GRAHAM. What is a cynic?
> LORD DARLINGTON. A man who knows the price of everything and the value of nothing.
> GRAHAM. And a sentimentalist, my dear Darlington, is a man who sees an absurd value in everything, and doesn't know the market price of any single thing.

Characters and characteristics — the psychological idea

The novelist H.G. Wells may have observed an unevenness of quality in Wilde's style, but Wilde has more often been criticised for displaying his brilliance as a wit at the expense of his skill as a dramatist. A critic writing in *Truth*, February 1895, complained of *The Importance of Being Earnest*, for example: 'There is no attempt in it at characterisation, but all the dramatis personae, from the heroes down to their butlers, talk pure and undiluted Wildese.' Even William Archer, a contemporary of Wilde who was generally enthusiastic about Wilde's plays, felt obliged to point out the dangers of Wilde's flair for coining brilliant and elegant witticisms for all of his characters: 'There are times when the output of Mr. Wilde's epigram factory threatens to become all trademark and no substance.' (*Theatrical World*, 1895) It is, perhaps, ironic that as a young man, in April 1883, Wilde should have written to Marie Prescott, an American actress: 'All good dialogue should give the effect of its being made by the reaction of the personages on one another. It should never seem to be ready made by the author.' (*Selected Letters*, p. 50)

Wilde certainly appreciated the importance of creating characters and crises which rang true in his plays of modern life, despite his assertion in *Intentions* that 'As a method Realism is a complete failure' and his contempt for the painstaking naturalism of playwrights such as Robertson. On 19 February 1892, he wrote to the Editor of the *Daily Telegraph*, discussing the relationship of

actors to the life of the play. Wilde was protesting at having had
his views misrepresented in an earlier article.

> What I really said was that the frame we call the stage was
> 'peopled with either living actors or moving puppets,' and I
> pointed out briefly, of necessity, that the personality of the
> actor is often a source of danger in the perfect representation
> of a work of art. It may distort. It may lead astray. It may be
> a discord in the tone or symphony. For anybody can act. [. . .]
> To act a particular part, however, is a very different thing, and
> a very difficult thing as well. [. . .] There are many advantages
> in puppets. They never argue. They have no crude views about
> art. [. . .] They recognise the presiding intellect of the dramatist,
> and have never been known to ask for their parts to be written
> up. [. . .] For modern plays, however, perhaps we had better
> have living players, for in modern plays actuality is everything.
> The charm − the ineffable charm − of the unreal is here
> denied us, and rightly. (*The Letters of Oscar Wilde*, p. 311)

So the effect he required in performance for a play like *Lady
Windermere's Fan* was an impression of 'actuality'; the characters
were not to appear simply as decorative and skilfully manipulated
marionettes. His decision to reshape the play so as to increase the
psychological interest of the characters also points to a serious
concern to give them *more* than a brilliant surface; the brilliance
was to be seen to be the expression of more deeply rooted feelings.

Some characters happily combine brilliance with feeling.
Mrs. Erlynne's wit and sophistication are consistent with her situation
and experience; they are not merely entertaining but demonstrate
the ways in which a woman of her intelligence and resilience has come
to terms with the mistakes of her past and the means by which she
plans to construct for herself a more successful future. It is important
for the audience to understand that the successes stem from the
character's needs and intentions rather than directly from Wilde's
delight in verbal display. As soon as Mrs. Erlynne appears, she admits
to a terror which she must overcome (p. 26):

> I am afraid of the women. You must introduce me to some of
> them. The men I can always manage.

We then see her pay successful court to Lady Jedburgh and appreciate
her poise because conscious of the strain we have been told it
conceals. It makes sense of Cecil Graham's remark (p. 27): 'That

woman can make one do anything she wants'. Mrs. Erlynne is the
pivotal character of the play. It is her arrival that moves the
Windermeres towards crisis; it is her action that saves the situation;
it is her need to reconcile her role as 'that woman' who has 'a past
before her' with her role as Lady Windermere's mother which
provides the serious strength of the play. She becomes a test case to
try the validity of that society's moral code.

Victorian society was intrigued and stimulated by the idea of a
'woman with a past'; such a character allowed the respectable theatre-
going public to speculate about the passions and pleasures of a life
of scandal, while at the same time confirming their perhaps self-
congratulatory conviction that such a life could lead only to despair
and that a conventional marriage, therefore, although in danger of
seeming dull, was the most desirable and acceptable condition of life
in a civilised society. Wilde used this pattern again in *A Woman of
No Importance* (1893), then worked variations on it in later plays:
in *An Ideal Husband*, for example, there is a woman who is as
sophisticated and reputedly scandalous as Mrs. Erlynne, but her past
is not itself the central issue – it is Sir Robert Chiltern, known as
a man of honour although in politics, who has a guilty secret in his
past which threatens to destroy him. Other Victorian dramatists
also used this theme effectively, especially Arthur Wing Pinero in
his play *The Second Mrs. Tanqueray*, which was first produced two
years after *Lady Windermere's Fan*.

In reply to a man who wrote enthusiastically about the New York
production of *Lady Windermere's Fan*, in February 1893, Wilde
explained his starting point and purpose in writing the play:

> The psychological idea that suggested the play is this. A woman
> who has had a child, but never known the passion of maternity
> (there are such women), suddenly sees the child she has
> abandoned falling over a precipice. There wakes in her the
> maternal feeling – the most terrible of all emotions – a thing
> that weak animals and little birds possess. She rushes to rescue,
> sacrifices herself, does follies – and the next day she feels 'This
> passion is too terrible. It wrecks my life. I don't want to know it
> again. It makes me suffer too much. Let me go away. I don't
> want to be a mother any more.' And so the fourth act is to me the
> psychological act, the act that is newest and most true. (*Letters
> of Oscar Wilde*, pp. 331-332)

Wilde uses the 'woman with a past' convention to give him a plot-line, but is concerned less with the events of the past than with the emotional life of the character out of which the events grew and the impact on the character of those events. Mrs. Erlynne is shown to be capable of development, learning from and being changed by experience, unlike the gallery of two-dimensional society portraits through which she moves (the Duchess of Berwick, Dumby, Cecil Graham and their like). Her initial mistake lies outside the immediate world of the play, in the past, but Wilde enables the audience to share in the experience it must have been by recreating it for Lady Windermere. Lady Windermere's rash decision to abandon her marriage becomes, therefore, a kind of dramatised exposition of Mrs. Erlynne's past as well as being an active element in the play's development. Wilde stresses the similarity between the two events (p. 38):

> MRS. ERLYNNE. Oh how terrible! The same words that twenty years ago I wrote to her father! and how bitterly I have been punished for it! No; my punishment, my real punishment is to-night, is now!

The spectacle of Lady Windermere's anguish, anger, remorse and terror reveals the pressures that could drive an intelligent and privileged woman — the woman Lord Windermere describes Mrs. Erlynne as having once been (p. 16) — to bring upon herself disgrace and exile. It also lends authority to Mrs. Erlynne's passionate pleading to her daughter to turn back from such a course of action, no matter what the provocation (p. 45):

> You don't know what may be in store for you, unless you leave this house at once. You don't know what it is to fall into the pit, to be despised, mocked, abandoned, sneered at — to be an outcast! to find the door shut against one, to have to creep in by hideous byways, afraid every moment lest the mask be stripped away from one's face, and all the while to hear the laughter, the horrible laughter of the world, a thing more tragic than all the tears the world has ever shed.

Two phrases here seem especially significant as a guide to Wilde's approach to the character: there is the nightmare of being 'an outcast' which makes even the resilient Mrs. Erlynne yearn desperately for acceptance by society (although she mocks the affectations and follies of that society); then there is the idea of the mask she must wear defensively but which she cannot trust to shield her when she most needs it. The vividness of the nightmare makes plain the reality of the self-sacrifice involved in her stepping out of concealment into the glare of the men's damning assumptions in order to preserve her daughter. Her terror of being stripped of the mask of cool sophistication she wears to face the world makes the brightness of her social manner poignant rather than purely 'Wildese'.

Lady Windermere's inability to cope with her situation is dramatically effective not only because her pathos engages the audience's sympathy but also as a telling contrast to Mrs. Erlynne's courage and panache. Mrs. Erlynne dominates and diminishes Lady Windermere — and all the rest of that fashionable world — so that the audience can feel the absurdity of such lightweight characters passing judgment on her. Mrs. Erlynne herself makes the point, not complacently but as an argument to convince her daughter of her need to stay safely within society's moral limits (p. 45):

> You — why, you are a mere girl, you would be lost. You haven't got the kind of brains that enables a woman to get back. You have neither the wit nor the courage.

Mrs. Erlynne understandably views the sanctity of marriage — Society's marriages — with some scepticism, particularly since the society that pays such emphatic lip-service to the idea is so often seen to be careless of the practice. Instead she turns to God and Motherhood as the foundations of a workable morality (p. 46): 'God gave you that child. He will require from you that you make his life fine, that you watch over him.' Lady Windermere's situation is simple; this duty to her child requires no real suffering so long as she trusts her husband, for he is a good man. But that, Mrs. Erlynne points out, is a bonus not a pre-condition of Lady Windermere's loyalty (p. 46):

> But even if he had a thousand loves, you must stay with your child. If he was harsh to you, you must stay with your child. If he ill-treated you, you must stay with your child. If he abandoned you, your place is with your child.

The insistent refrain which hammers home the moral perhaps seems absurdly rhetorical, but Wilde relies on the dramatic intensity of the moment and the audience's consciousness of the price Mrs. Erlynne is paying for her new moral certainties to justify the heightened style.

This enlightenment comes, not at the end of the play, but in Act Three — so what is left for her in Act Four, that act which Wilde declared

was 'the psychological act, the newest and most true'? There is the
expected reward for her heroic protection of her daughter's honour —
marriage to Lord Augustus. But, more interestingly, there is the
difficulty she has in coming to terms with the new idea she now has
of herself as a mother, a woman capable of impulsive unselfishness,
a woman capable of love. This presents Wilde with the problem of
how to preserve the vitality and wit of the character, which set her
apart from more conventional women, while at the same time
making convincing her newly found virtues. It would have been
easy for the sudden flowering of her maternal instincts to have
softened Mrs. Erlynne's style into sentimentality, but her unsettling
discovery of a motive more powerful than self-interest is all the
more persuasive because Wilde chooses not to whitewash her
characteristic self-assertion (p. 64):

> I have no ambition to play the part of a mother. Only once in
> my life have I known a mother's feelings. That was last night.
> They were terrible — they made me suffer — they made me suffer
> too much. For twenty years, as you say, I have lived childless, —
> I want to live childless still. (*Hiding her feelings with a trivial
> laugh.*) [. . .] I lost one illusion last night. I thought I had no
> heart. I find I have, and a heart doesn't suit me, Windermere.
> Somehow it doesn't go with modern dress. It makes one look
> old. (*Takes up hand-mirror from table and looks into it.*) And
> it spoils one's career at critical moments.

The audience are able to judge Lord Windermere's blindness and feel
pleased with their own superior understanding of the situation. They
can enjoy the niceness of Lady Windermere's grateful admiration for
the woman they know to be her mother and be content that she remains
in childlike ignorance of the whole truth. They will relish the prospect
of the dance Mrs. Erlynne will lead her new husband and be relieved
that the tricky question of whether or not she should be re-admitted
into polite society has been neatly resolved to the satisfaction of
those who feel that true contrition should be rewarded as well as
of those who insist that 'women who have committed what the
world calls a fault' (p. 6) should be forever barred from that world.

Wilde's first title for the play was *A Good Woman*; there are
several discussions of what qualities make a good woman and whether
Mrs. Erlynne is or is not 'good'. It is **Lady Windermere** who at first
seems the more probable subject of *A Good Woman* and, certainly,
the play does explore that idea of her as well as of her mother.

As far as society is concerned, Lady Windermere is a paragon, 'good' without doubt. It is she that Lord Darlington thinks of when he says (p. 52): 'This woman has purity and innocence. She has everything we men have lost.' She seems to stand above all other women in his experience (p. 51): 'She is a good woman. She is the only good woman I have ever met in my life.' The sincerity of his admiration is not only a tribute to her, it is also proof of his moral superiority over the others of his acquaintance who have no appreciation of such qualities but live life entirely on its polished surface, Cecil Graham, for example (p. 52):

> CECIL GRAHAM (*lighting a cigarette*). Well, you are a lucky fellow! Why, I have met hundreds of good women. I never seem to meet any but good women. The world is perfectly packed with good women. To know them is a middle-class education. [. . .] My dear fellow, what on earth should we men do going about with purity and innocence? A carefully thought-out buttonhole is much more effective.

Lady Windermere's respectability is generally recognised and her judgments taken as authoritative on matters of social propriety; for instance, Lord Augustus's anxieties about Mrs. Erlynne are dispersed when he learns that Mrs. Erlynne is to be a guest at Lady Windermere's house. She takes herself and her virtue very seriously, as is immediately apparent in the opening conversation with Lord Darlington (pp. 2-7).

> LADY WINDERMERE. Well, I have something of the Puritan in me. I was brought up like that. I am glad of it. [. . .] Nowadays people seem to look on life as a speculation. It is not a speculation. It is a sacrament. Its ideal is Love. Its purification is sacrifice.

The style of her speech here is rigid and trenchant, a series of short, sharp statements without qualifying or softening clauses. Wilde uses Lord Darlington's responses to alert the audience to the dangers and absurdities in her attitude, but Lady Windermere is unassailable in her certainties. He warns her (p. 5):

> LORD DARLINGTON. Do you know I am afraid that good people do a great deal of harm in this world. Certainly the greatest harm they do is that they make badness of such extraordinary importance.

After she has refused her husband's plea that she should allow
Mrs. Erlynne to have 'a chance of a happier, a surer life than she has
had' (p. 17), she lays down the law on matters which she has neither
the wisdom nor the experience of life to pass judgment on (p. 17):

> LORD WINDERMERE. Won't you help a woman who is trying
>   to get back?
> LADY WINDERMERE. No! If a woman really repents, she never
>   wishes to return to the society that has made or seen her ruin.

What of Christian charity? Lady Windermere has to learn through
experience what she lacks the imagination and compassion to
appreciate otherwise. It is her progress towards enlightenment that
marks out the boundaries of the play, leaving out anything which
does not directly relate to that line of development. For example,
we do not *see* her child; it is enough to have it present as an idea.
Similarly, once Lord Darlington has served his purpose in her learning
process, he is dismissed to a kind of exile abroad; it is enough that
he has been instrumental in her recognition that 'There is a bitter
irony in things, a bitter irony in the way we talk of good and bad
women . . .' (p. 57). She is finally able to instruct her husband in the
true morality to which he has become suddenly blind (p. 58):

> Arthur, Arthur, don't talk so bitterly about any woman. I don't
> think now that people can be divided into the good and the bad
> as though they were two separate races or creations. What are
> called good women may have terrible things in them, mad moods
> of recklessness, assertion, jealousy, sin. Bad women, as they
> are termed, may have in them sorrow, repentance, pity, sacrifice.

She is rewarded with the promise of future happiness with her
husband and child, beginning at Selby, where 'the roses are white
and red' (p. 71). Wilde is prepared to allow her to sink into a kind
of sentimentality at the end which answers her sanctimoniousness
at the beginning. The difficulty with this character is in making her
attractive enough to engage the audience's sympathy; while looking
for her to grow out of her adolescent self-righteousness, the audience
need to desire her happiness and to understand the high value others
place upon her.

   Lady Windermere's appeal may, in performance, be presented
persuasively by the charm of the actress playing the part; in the text,
it is demonstrated by the ability she appears to have to inspire love
and selfless devotion in others.

Lord Darlington's role in the play is primarily to test Lady Windermere's ability to stick to her convictions and her husband in the face of strong temptation and distress. It is important that he should be a possible alternative to Lord Windermere, the kind of man capable of tempting Lady Windermere to abandon all she has stood for. He must be different from the other eligible bachelors yet able to shine in their world. Thus Wilde allows him to affect the graceful insouciance of the fashionable beau (p. 7):

> As a wicked man I am a complete failure. Why, there are lots of people who say I have never really done anything wrong in the whole course of my life. Of course they only say it behind my back.

Lady Windermere is unimpressed (p. 8): 'Lord Darlington is trivial'. However, from the beginning it is made clear that beneath this cultivated charm beats a heart capable of serious passion and a sense of honour which is challenging because it does not merely follow the pattern of the age. He carefully and gently prepares Lady Windermere for the shock of discovering her husband's apparent infidelity, but does not press his own claim to her affection when she shrinks from the idea of seeking consolation outside marriage. Once she has declared her disgust and sense of betrayal at her husband's relationship with Mrs. Erlynne, he explains the code of conduct that had inhibited him earlier (p. 30): 'I couldn't! A man can't tell these things about another man!' Lord Darlington is not a cad! However, he genuinely believes that Lord Windermere has sacrificed any right to such discreet loyalty by insisting on bringing his mistress into his wife's home. Released from his honourable silence, Lord Darlington can freely and passionately plead for Lady Windermere's love. His declaration may, in the long run, be seen to be misguided, but Wilde makes it immediately attractive. Lord Darlington will incur the condemnation of Society too, even if not as terribly as Lady Windermere. He offers her (p. 31):

> My life — my whole life. Take it, and do with it what you will . . . I love you — love you as I have never loved any living thing.

He does not try to deceive her about the cost of such defiance of society's conventions (p. 31):

> I won't tell you that the world matters nothing, or the world's voice, or the voice of society. They matter far too much. But there

are moments when one has to choose between living one's own
life, fully, entirely, completely — or dragging out some false,
shallow, degrading existence that the world in its hypocrisy
demands. You have that moment now. Choose! Oh, my love,
choose.

It is important that the choice should seem to be a real one, that
what Lord Darlington offers is a viable alternative to what Lady
Windermere would be leaving, otherwise the whole drama appears
merely a confection with the outcome ponderously predictable,
incapable of creating suspense or surprise. His questioning of
received ideas about right and wrong, similarly, must demand
serious attention rather than be conspicuoulsy misguided (p. 31):

Wrong? What is wrong? It's wrong for a man to abandon his
wife for a shameless woman. It is wrong for a wife to remain
with a man who so dishonours her.

The force of his argument is dissipated as soon as the audience know
that Lord Windermere has not betrayed his wife, that it is *her* trust
in him that has faltered not *his* faithfulness to her. After that, all that
is left for Lord Darlington is to accept his disappointment with
gentlemanly grace. He does not reproach Lady Windermere for
raising his hopes only to dash them; he speaks with poetic generosity
of her refusal to succumb to his wooing (p. 51): 'We are all in the
gutter, but some of us are looking at the stars'. Even when he has
nothing to gain from fidelity and risks the mockery of his friends,
he speaks earnestly of his feelings (p. 53):

Cecil, if one really loves a woman, all other women in the world
become absolutely meaningless to one. Love changes one — *I*
am changed.

Wilde allows no witty undermining of this declaration; Cecil Graham
merely slides away from such an embarrassingly direct display of
feeling, as if outmanoeuvred by it. Lord Darlington is not diminished.
Nonetheless, once Lady Windermere has discovered that even she is
fallible and been taught that a mother may never become another
man's mistress, no matter what the provocation, then there is no
rôle left for Lord Darlington to play with honour or wit, and he is
not to be allowed to embarrass Lady Windermere by haunting the
scenes of her newly won happiness. He sticks to his plan to leave

England for a voluntary exile, but without the companionship of the woman he loves. Arguably he is properly punished for even contemplating running off with another man's wife. As Mrs. Erlynne says: 'One pays for one's sin, and then one pays again, and all one's life one pays' (p. 45).

Lord Windermere is a man of honour, unwaveringly true to his wife, a man of good intentions and strong convictions. It is his misfortune to be misunderstood or mistaken at almost every point in the play. At the beginning, his honourable attempts to help his wife's mother without hurting his wife's cherished illusions are misunderstood so that he appears faithless and crass. His defence of Mrs. Erlynne is delivered under the shadow of his supposed passion for her. His desperate cry for help and counsel is heard only by the audience. In Lord Darlington's rooms he appears morose and graceless among the polished attitudes of Dumby, Cecil Graham and even Lord Darlington, his presence agonising for the audience who are anxious about Lady Windermere. His outrage after the discovery of his wife's fan seems both threatening and ill-timed, and his subsequent contempt for Mrs. Erlynne is known by the audience and by his wife to be mistaken. When he strokes his wife's hair and calls her 'Child' (p. 70), the gesture is in danger of appearing absurdly patronising in view of his insistent misinterpretation of the situation. All this could be counteracted by a sympathetic and attractive performance from an actor who could more than justify Lady Windermere's love for her husband and Mrs. Erlynne's spirited defence of him (pp. 44-46) and who could make the audience rejoice at the play's happy ending. Wilde's Victorian audience would have had a more immediate understanding of Lord Windermere's dilemma than would late twentieth-century playgoers. For Wilde's contemporaries Lord Windermere could represent the values underpinning their society: good breeding, good manners, good income, an unswerving devotion to his wife and child, combining conventional principles with respectable passions.

Since being or not being accepted by 'this demmed thing called Society' (p. 23) is crucial to the play's action and arguments, its presentation of that society is important. The four main characters inhabit a world that would have been familiar to the audience at the St. James's Theatre in 1892, so that Wilde could rely on that audience to fill out the details and background of the portraits he sketched. Wilde's satire holds up to ridicule the follies, affectations or vices of Society by presenting the familiar in a slightly unusual perspective

or by exaggerating certain elements so as to render the whole picture
grotesque or at least absurd. Thus **Cecil Graham** and **Dumby** are
recognisably young men of good family and adequate income, with a
taste for witty conversation, card-playing, drinking and flirtation.
They are without responsibilities as yet, so do not become involved
in serious moral issues; this both explains and excuses their
relentless flippancy and irreverence. Their enjoyment of conversation
is entertaining, giving Wilde scope to display his own 'undiluted
Wildese', and is attractive when the wit is not spiteful. However,
Wilde does draw attention to the idleness, insincerity and occasional
malice of their attitudes. Lady Windermere has little respect for them
and requires Lord Darlington to be better (p. 3): 'But I shouldn't
like you at all if I thought you were what most other men are'.
When they cannot resist the temptation to make suggestive remarks
about Mrs. Erlynne, Lord Windermere rebukes them firmly (p. 50):

> Dumby, you are ridiculous, and Cecil, you let your tongue run
> away with you. You must leave Mrs. Erlynne alone. You don't
> really know anything about her, and you're always talking
> scandal against her.

They are unabashed. Nonetheless, the power they have to cause pain
is vividly expressed in Mrs. Erlynne's outcry against 'the horrible
laughter of the world' (p. 45). Similarly, the **Duchess of Berwick** is
amusing so long as she is not visibly destructive of the happiness or
tranquillity of others. She shows the same concerns as any
conscientious mother in Society, namely a preoccupation with
appearances and a determination to marry her daughter off with as
little trouble as possible to an acceptable man – that is, a man of
considerable wealth and a proper recognition that it will be his
mother-in-law who organises his life thereafter. Yet the snobbery,
the callousness and the complacent ignorance of her kind are
ridiculed by Wilde. Her concern to protect her young daughter from
knowledge of the wicked ways of the world and to ensure a secure
future for her, far from seeming as selfless as Mrs. Erlynne's maternal
impulse, appears self-assertive and suffocating – the proof of that
is in the mindless insipidity of her daughter. Since the audience
have no reason to feel especially interested in young Agatha, they
can watch with amusement as her mother briskly marshals her and
'one of Nature's gentlemen', the wealthy but lamentably Australian
Mr. Hopper, into an engagement. The humour comes in part from the
way Wilde makes her so forcefully unaware of her own insensitivity

and hypocrisy. She is heavily patronising about Australia (p. 21):
'It must be so pretty with all the dear little kangaroos flying about.
[. . .] However, it is a very young country, isn't it?' Until the idea
of Australia becomes inconveniently intrusive (p. 34):

> Oh, don't mention that dreadful vulgar place. [. . .] I think on
> the whole that Grosvenor Square would be a more healthy place
> to reside in. There are lots of vulgar people living in Grosvenor
> Square, but at any rate there are no horrid kangaroos crawling
> about.

She remains sturdily unaware of any inconsistencies or crassness in
her words; the audience laugh *at* rather than *with* her. However,
her insensitive interference in the lives of others is shown to be
destructive in Act One, when she comes to tell Lady Windermere
of the gossip concerning her husband. Insisting on her loathing
of scandal and her wish to be a friend to Lady Windermere, she
vigorously and enthusiastically undermines the Windermere
marriage. The fact that the scandal she brings is merely scandal
and not the truth makes her meddling particularly unpleasant.
She throws a most unattractive light upon the interests and ideas
of her world (pp. 10-13); there is pleasure in finding weakness in
a man well-known for his integrity ('Only last night at dear Lady
Jansen's every one was saying how extraordinary it was that, of all
men in London, Windermere should behave in such a way') and
a deadening assumption that all marriages must involve betrayal
and compromise, no matter how promising the start.

Lord Augustus, the Duchess's brother, is more affectionately
treated; he hurts no-one. His role is, in part, to provide a solution
to the problem of what is to be done about Mrs. Erlynne. In no way
will theirs be a marriage of equals, but what he lacks in wit he makes
up for in wealth and social status. He is not clever enough to resent
Mrs. Erlynne's manipulation of him so may be expected to live
happily enough with her. He is also the good-natured butt of his
friends' wit, only occasionally goaded into protest (p. 49):

> LORD AUGUSTUS. You're getting annoying, dear boy; you're
> getting demmed annoying.
> CECIL GRAHAM. Now, Tuppy, you've lost your figure and
> you've lost your character. Don't lose your temper; you have
> only got one.

Further reading

Collections of Wilde's writings:

Plays, Prose Writings, and Poems (London, Dent: Everyman's
   Library)
   Contains *The Importance of Being Earnest* and *Lady Windermere's
   Fan* as well as *The Picture of Dorian Gray*, *The Ballad of Reading
   Gaol* and the essays 'The Critic as Artist' and 'The Soul of Man
   Under Socialism'.

Three Plays (London, Methuen: Master Playwrights)
   Contains *An Ideal Husband* and *Lady Windermere's Fan* as well
   as *Importance* with additional material from the Fourth Act.
   Introduction by H. Montgomery Hyde.

Portable Oscar Wilde (Harmondsworth, Penguin: Viking Portable
   Library).

De Profundis (Harmondsworth, Penguin: Penguin English Library).

Lord Arthur Savile's Crime and Other Stories (Harmondsworth,
   Penguin: Modern Classics).

General biographical background

Oscar Wilde by H. Montgomery Hyde (London, Methuen Paperbacks)

Oscar Wilde by Philippe Jullian (London, Constable)

Selected Letters of Oscar Wilde, edited by Rupert Hart-Davis
   (Oxford University Press)

Son of Oscar Wilde by Vyvyan Holland (London, Hart-Davis).

General critical studies

Oscar Wilde by James Laver (British Council).

Oscar Wilde: A Collection of Critical Essays, edited by Richard
   Ellmann (Englewood Cliffs, Prentice-Hall).

Last Theatres 1904-1910 by Max Beerbohm (London, Hart-Davis)

Lady Windermere's Fan

Lady Windermere's Fan was first performed at the St. James's Theatre, London, under the management of Mr. George Alexander on 22 February 1892 with the following cast:

LORD WINDERMERE	Mr. George Alexander
LORD DARLINGTON	Mr Nutcombe Gould
LORD AUGUSTUS LORTON	Mr. H.H. Vincent
MR. CECIL GRAHAM	Mr. Ben Webster
MR. DUMBY	Mr. Vane-Tempest
MR. HOPPER	Mr. Alfred Holles
PARKER (Butler)	Mr. V. Sansbury
LADY WINDERMERE	Miss Lily Hanbury
THE DUCHESS OF BERWICK	Miss Fanny Coleman
LADY AGATHA CARLISLE	Miss Laura Graves
LADY PLYMDALE	Miss Granville
LADY JEDBURGH	Miss B. Page
LADY STUTFIELD	Miss Madge Girdlestone
MRS. COWPER-COWPER	Miss A. de Winton
MRS. ERLYNNE	Miss Marion Terry
ROSALIE (Maid)	Miss Winifred Dolan

THE SCENES OF THE PLAY

ACT I	Morning-room in Lord Windermere's house
ACT II	Drawing-room in Lord Windermere's house.
ACT III	Lord Darlington's rooms.
ACT IV	Same as Act I.
TIME:	The Present
PLACE:	London.

The action of the play takes place within twenty-four hours, beginning on a Tuesday afternoon at five o'clock, and ending the next day at 1.30 p.m.

First Act

SCENE

Morning-room of Lord Windermere's house in Carlton House Terrace. Doors C. and R. Bureau with books and papers R. Sofa with small tea-table L. Window opening on to terrace L. Table R.

LADY WINDERMERE *is at table R., arranging roses in a blue bowl.*

Enter PARKER.

PARKER. Is your ladyship at home this afternoon?

LADY WINDERMERE. Yes—who has called?

PARKER. Lord Darlington, my lady.

LADY WINDERMERE (*hesitates for a moment*). Show him up—and I'm at home to any one who calls.

PARKER. Yes, my lady. (*Exit C.*)

LADY WINDERMERE. It's best for me to see him before to-night. I'm glad he's come.

Enter PARKER *C.*

PARKER. Lord Darlington.

Enter LORD DARLINGTON *C.*

Exit PARKER.

LORD DARLINGTON. How do you do, Lady Windermere?

LADY WINDERMERE. How do you do, Lord Darlington? No, I can't shake hands with you. My hands are all wet with these roses. Aren't they lovely? They came up from Selby this morning.

LORD DARLINGTON. They are quite perfect. (*Sees a fan lying on the table.*) And what a wonderful fan! May I look at it?

LADY WINDERMERE. Do. Pretty, isn't it! It's got my name on it, and everything. I have only just seen it myself. It's my husband's birthday present to me. You know to-day is my birthday?

LORD DARLINGTON. No? Is it really?

LADY WINDERMERE. Yes, I'm of age to-day. Quite an important day in my life, isn't it? That is why I am giving this party to-night. Do sit down. (*Still arranging flowers.*)

LORD DARLINGTON (*sitting down*). I wish I had known it was your birthday, Lady Windermere. I would have covered the whole street in front of your house with flowers for you to walk on. They are made for you.

A short pause.

LADY WINDERMERE. Lord Darlington, you annoyed me last night at the Foreign Office. I am afraid you are going to annoy me again.

LORD DARLINGTON. I, Lady Windermere?

Enter PARKER *and* FOOTMAN *C., with tray and tea things.*

LADY WINDERMERE. Put it there, Parker. That will do. (*Wipes her hands with her pocket-handkerchief, goes to teatable L., and sits down.*) Won't you come over, Lord Darlington?

Exit PARKER *C.*

LORD DARLINGTON (*takes chair and goes across L.C.*). I am

quite miserable, Lady Windermere. You must tell me what I did. (*Sits down at table L.*)

LADY WINDERMERE. Well, you kept paying me elaborate compliments the whole evening.

LORD DARLINGTON (*smiling*). Ah, nowadays we are all of us so hard up, that the only pleasant things to pay *are* compliments. They're the only things we *can* pay.

LADY WINDERMERE (*shaking her head*). No, I am talking very seriously. You mustn't laugh, I am quite serious. I don't like compliments, and I don't see why a man should think he is pleasing a woman enormously when he says to her a whole heap of things that he doesn't mean.

LORD DARLINGTON. Ah, but I did mean them. (*Takes tea which she offers him.*)

LADY WINDERMERE (*gravely*). I hope not. I should be sorry to have to quarrel with you, Lord Darlington. I like you very much, you know that. But I shouldn't like you at all if I thought you were what most other men are. Believe me, you are better than most other men, and I sometimes think you pretend to be worse.

LORD DARLINGTON. We all have our little vanities, Lady Windermere.

LADY WINDERMERE. Why do you make that your special one? (*Still seated at table L.*)

LORD DARLINGTON (*still seated L.C.*). Oh, nowadays so many conceited people go about Society pretending to be good, that I think it shows rather a sweet and modest disposition to pretend to be bad. Besides, there is this to be said. If you pretend to be good, the world takes you very seriously. If you pretend to be bad, it doesn't. Such is the astounding stupidity of optimism.

LADY WINDERMERE. Don't you *want* the world to take you seriously then, Lord Darlington?

LORD DARLINGTON. No, not the world. Who are the people the world takes seriously? All the dull people one can think of, from the Bishops down to the bores. I should like *you* to take me very seriously, Lady Windermere, *you* more than any one else in life.

LADY WINDERMERE. Why—why me?

LORD DARLINGTON (*after a slight hesitation*). Because I think we might be great friends. Let us be great friends. You may want a friend some day.

LADY WINDERMERE. Why do you say that?

LORD DARLINGTON. Oh!—we all want friends at times.

LADY WINDERMERE. I think we're very good friends already, Lord Darlington. We can always remain so as long as you don't——

LORD DARLINGTON. Don't what?

LADY WINDERMERE. Don't spoil it by saying extravagant silly things to me. You think I am a Puritan, I suppose? Well, I have something of the Puritan in me. I was brought up like that. I am glad of it. My mother died when I was a mere child. I lived always with Lady Julia, my father's elder sister, you know. She was stern to me, but she taught me what the world is forgetting, the difference that there is between what is right and what is wrong. *She* allowed of no compromise. *I* allow of none.

LORD DARLINGTON. My dear Lady Windermere!

LADY WINDERMERE (*leaning back on the sofa*). You look on me as being behind the age.—Well, I am! I should be sorry to be on the same level as an age like this.

LORD DARLINGTON. You think the age very bad?

LADY WINDERMERE. Yes. Nowadays people seem to look on life as a speculation. It is not a speculation. It is a sacrament. Its ideal is Love. Its purification is sacrifice.

LORD DARLINGTON (*smiling*). Oh, anything is better than being sacrificed!

LADY WINDERMERE (*leaning forward*). Don't say that.

LORD DARLINGTON. I do say it. I feel it—I know it.

Enter PARKER *C.*

PARKER. The men want to know if they are to put the carpets on the terrace for to-night, my lady?

LADY WINDERMERE. You don't think it will rain, Lord Darlington, do you?

LORD DARLINGTON. I won't hear of its raining on your birthday!

LADY WINDERMERE. Tell them to do it at once, Parker.

Exit PARKER *C.*

LORD DARLINGTON (*still seated*). Do you think then—of course I am only putting an imaginary instance—do you think that in the case of a young married couple, say about two years married, if the husband suddenly becomes the intimate friend of a woman of—well, more than doubtful character—is always calling upon her, lunching with her, and probably paying her bills—do you think that the wife should not console herself?

LADY WINDERMERE (*frowning*). Console herself?

LORD DARLINGTON. Yes, I think she should—I think she has the right.

LADY WINDERMERE. Because the husband is vile—should the wife be vile also?

LORD DARLINGTON. Vileness is a terrible word, Lady Windermere.

LADY WINDERMERE. It is a terrible thing. Lord Darlington.

LORD DARLINGTON. Do you know I am afraid that good people do a great deal of harm in this world. Certainly the greatest harm they do is that they make badness of such extraordinary importance. It is absurd to divide people into good and bad. People are either charming or tedious. I take the side of the charming, and you, Lady Windermere, can't help belonging to them.

LADY WINDERMERE. Now, Lord Darlington. (*Rising and crossing R., front of him.*) Don't stir, I am merely going to finish my flowers. (*Goes to table R.C.*)

LORD DARLINGTON (*rising and moving chair*). And I must say I think you are very hard on modern life, Lady Windermere. Of course there is much against it, I admit. Most women, for instance, nowadays, are rather mercenary.

LADY WINDERMERE. Don't talk about such people.

LORD DARLINGTON. Well then, setting aside mercenary people, who, of course, are dreadful, do you think seriously that women who have committed what the world calls a fault should never be forgiven?

LADY WINDERMERE (*standing at table*). I think they should never be forgiven.

LORD DARLINGTON. And men? Do you think that there should be the same laws for men as there are for women?

LADY WINDERMERE. Certainly!

LORD DARLINGTON. I think life too complex a thing to be settled by these hard and fast rules.

LADY WINDERMERE. If we had 'these hard and fast rules,' we should find life much more simple.

LORD DARLINGTON. You allow of no exceptions?

LADY WINDERMERE. None!

LORD DARLINGTON. Ah, what a fascinating Puritan you are, Lady Windermere!

LADY WINDERMERE. The adjective was unnecessary, Lord Darlington.

LORD DARLINGTON. I couldn't help it. I can resist everything except temptation.

LADY WINDERMERE. You have the modern affectation of weakness.

LORD DARLINGTON (*looking at her*). It's only an affectation, Lady Windermere.

Enter PARKER *C.*

PARKER. The Duchess of Berwick and Lady Agatha Carlisle.

Enter the DUCHESS OF BERWICK *and* LADY AGATHA CARLISLE *C.*

Exit PARKER *C.*

DUCHESS OF BERWICK (*coming down C., and shaking hands*). Dear Margaret, I am so pleased to see you. You remember Agatha, don't you? (*Crossing L.C.*) How do you do, Lord Darlington? I won't let you know my daughter, you are far too wicked.

LORD DARLINGTON. Don't say that, Duchess. As a wicked man I am a complete failure. Why, there are lots of people who say I have never really done anything wrong in the whole course of my life. Of course they only say it behind my back.

DUCHESS OF BERWICK. Isn't he dreadful? Agatha, this is Lord Darlington. Mind you don't believe a word he says. (LORD DARLINGTON *crosses R.C.*) No, no tea, thank you, dear. (*Crosses and sits on sofa.*) We have just had tea at Lady Markby's. Such bad tea, too. It was quite undrinkable. I wasn't at all surprised. Her own son-in-law supplies it. Agatha is looking forward so much to your ball to-night, dear Margaret.

LADY WINDERMERE (*seated L.C.*). Oh, you mustn't think it is going to be a ball, Duchess. It is only a dance in honour of my birthday. A small and early.

LORD DARLINGTON (*standing L.C.*). Very small, very early, and very select, Duchess.

DUCHESS OF BERWICK (*on sofa L.*). Of course it's going to be select. But we know *that*, dear Margaret, about *your* house. It is really one of the few houses in London where I can take Agatha, and where I feel perfectly secure about dear Berwick. I don't know what society is coming to. The most dreadful people seem to go everywhere. They certainly come to my parties—the men get quite furious if one doesn't ask them. Really, some one should make a stand against it.

LADY WINDERMERE. I will, Duchess. I will have no one in my house about whom there is any scandal.

LORD DARLINGTON (*R.C.*). Oh, don't say that, Lady Windermere. I should never be admitted! (*Sitting.*)

DUCHESS OF BERWICK. Oh, men don't matter. With women it is different. We're good. Some of us are, at least. But we are positively getting elbowed into the corner. Our husbands would really forget our existence if we didn't nag at them from time to time, just to remind them that we have a perfect legal right to do so.

LORD DARLINGTON. It's a curious thing, Duchess, about the game of marriage—a game, by the way, that is going out of fashion—the wives hold all the honours, and invariably lose the odd trick.

DUCHESS OF BERWICK. The odd trick? Is that the husband, Lord Darlington?

LORD DARLINGTON. It would be rather a good name for the modern husband.

DUCHESS OF BERWICK. Dear Lord Darlington, how thoroughly depraved you are!

LADY WINDERMERE. Lord Darlington is trivial.

LORD DARLINGTON. Ah, don't say that, Lady Windermere.

LADY WINDERMERE. Why do you *talk* so trivially about life, then?

LORD DARLINGTON. Because I think that life is far too important a thing ever to talk seriously about it. (*Moves up C.*)

DUCHESS OF BERWICK. What does he mean? Do, as a concession to my poor wits, Lord Darlington, just explain to
me what you really mean.

LORD DARLINGTON (*coming down back of table*). I think I had
better not, Duchess. Nowadays to be intelligible is to be
found out. Good-bye! (*Shakes hands with* DUCHESS.) And
now—(*goes up stage*) Lady Windermere, good-bye. I may
come to-night, mayn't I? Do let me come.

LADY WINDERMERE (*standing up stage with* LORD DARLING-
TON). Yes, certainly. But you are not to say foolish, insincere
things to people.

LORD DARLINGTON (*smiling*). Ah! you are beginning to
reform me. It is a dangerous thing to reform any one, Lady
Windermere. (*Bows, and exit C.*)

DUCHESS OF BERWICK (*who has risen, goes C.*). What a
charming, wicked creature. I like him so much. I'm quite
delighted he's gone! How sweet you're looking! Where *do*
you get your gowns? And now I must tell you how sorry I
am for you, dear Margaret. (*Crosses to sofa and sits with*
LADY WINDERMERE.) Agatha, darling!

LADY AGATHA. Yes, mamma. (*Rises.*)

DUCHESS OF BERWICK. Will you go and look over the
photograph album that I see there?

LADY AGATHA. Yes, mamma. (*Goes to table up L.*)

DUCHESS OF BERWICK. Dear girl! She is so found of photo-
graphs of Switzerland. Such a pure taste, I think. But I
really am so sorry for you, Margaret.

LADY WINDERMERE (*smiling*). Why, Duchess?

DUCHESS OF BERWICK. Oh, on account of that horrid
woman. She dresses so well, too, which makes it much
worse, sets such a dreadful example. Augustus—you know
my disreputable brother—such a trial to us all—well,
Augustus is completely infatuated about her. It is quite
scandalous, for she is absolutely inadmissible into society.

Many a woman has a past, but I am told that she has at least a dozen, and that they all fit.

LADY WINDERMERE. Whom are you talking about, Duchess?

DUCHESS OF BERWICK. About Mrs. Erlynne.

LADY WINDERMERE. Mrs. Erlynne? I never heard of her, Duchess. And what *has* she to do with me?

DUCHESS OF BERWICK. My poor child! Agatha, darling!

LADY AGATHA. Yes, mamma.

DUCHESS OF BERWICK. Will you go out on the terrace and look at the sunset?

LADY AGATHA. Yes, mamma. (*Exit through window L.*)

DUCHESS OF BERWICK. Sweet girl! So devoted to sunsets! Shows such refinement of feeling, does it not? After all, there is nothing like Nature, is there?

LADY WINDERMERE. But what is it, Duchess? Why do you talk to me about this person?

DUCHESS OF BERWICK. Don't you really know? I assure you we're all so distressed about it. Only last night at dear Lady Jansen's every one was saying how extraordinary it was that, of all men in London, Windermere should behave in such a way.

LADY WINDERMERE. My husband—what has *he* got to do with any woman of that kind?

DUCHESS OF BERWICK. Ah, what indeed, dear? That is the point. He goes to see her continually, and stops for hours at a time, and while he is there she is not at home to any one. Not that many ladies call on her, dear, but she has a great many disreputable men friends—my own brother particularly, as I told you—and that is what makes it so dreadful about Windermere. We looked upon *him* as being such a model husband, but I am afraid there is no doubt about it. My dear nieces—you know the Saville girls, don't you?— such nice domestic creatures—plain, dreadfully plain, but

so good—well, they're always at the window doing fancy
work, and making ugly things for the poor, which I think
so useful of them in these dreadful socialistic days, and this
terrible woman has taken a house in Curzon Street, right
opposite them—such a respectable street, too! I don't know
what we're coming to! And they tell me that Windermere
goes there four and five times a week—they *see* him. They
can't help it—and although they never talk scandal, they—
well, of course—they remark on it to every one. And the
worst of it all is that I have been told that this woman has
got a great deal of money out of somebody, for it seems that
she came to London six months ago without anything at all
to speak of, and now she has this charming house in Mayfair,
drives her ponies in the Park every afternoon and all—well,
all—since she has known poor dear Windermere.

LADY WINDERMERE. Oh, I can't believe it!

DUCHESS OF BERWICK. But it's quite true, my dear. The
whole of London knows it. That is why I felt it was better
to come and talk to you, and advise you to take Windermere
away at once to Homburg or to Aix, where he'll have something to amuse him, and where you can watch him all day
long. I assure you, my dear, that on several occasions after
I was first married, I had to pretend to be very ill, and was
obliged to drink the most unpleasant mineral waters, merely
to get Berwick out of town. He was so extremely susceptible.
Though I am bound to say he never gave away any large
sums of money to anybody. He is far too high-principled
for that!

LADY WINDERMERE (*interrupting*). Duchess, Duchess, it's
impossible! (*Rising and crossing stage to C.*) We are only
married two years. Our child is but six months old. (*Sits in
chair R. of L. table.*)

DUCHESS OF BERWICK. Ah, the dear pretty baby! How is
the little darling? Is it a boy or a girl? I hope a girl—Ah, no,

I remember it's a boy! I'm so sorry. Boys are so wicked. My boy is excessively immoral. You wouldn't believe at what hours he comes home. And he's only left Oxford a few months—I really don't know what they teach them there.

LADY WINDERMERE. Are *all* men bad?

DUCHESS OF BERWICK. Oh, all of them, my dear, all of them, without any exception. And they never grow any better. Men become old, but they never become good.

LADY WINDERMERE. Windermere and I married for love.

DUCHESS OF BERWICK. Yes, we begin like that. It was only Berwick's brutal and incessant threats of suicide that made me accept him at all, and before the year was out, he was running after all kinds of petticoats, every colour, every shape, every material. In fact, before the honeymoon was over, I caught him winking at my maid, a most pretty, respectable girl. I dismissed her at once without a character.— No, I remember I passed her on to my sister; poor dear Sir George is so short-sighted, I thought it wouldn't matter. But it did, though—it was most unfortunate. (*Rises.*) And now, my dear child, I must go, as we are dining out. And mind you don't take this little aberration of Windermere's too much to heart. Just take him abroad, and he'll come back to you all right.

LADY WINDERMERE. Come back to me? (*C.*)

DUCHESS OF BERWICK (*L.C.*). Yes, dear, these wicked women get our husbands away from us, but they always come back, slightly damaged, of course. And don't make scenes, men hate them!

LADY WINDERMERE. It is very kind of you, Duchess, to come and tell me all this. But I can't believe that my husband is untrue to me.

DUCHESS OF BERWICK. Pretty child! I was like that once. Now I know that all men are monsters. (LADY WINDERMERE *rings bell.*) The only thing to do is to feed the wretches well.

A good cook does wonders, and that I know you have. My dear Margaret, you are not going to cry?

LADY WINDERMERE. You needn't be afraid, Duchess, I never cry.

DUCHESS OF BERWICK. That's quite right, dear. Crying is the refuge of plain women but the ruin of pretty ones. Agatha, darling.

LADY AGATHA (*entering L.*). Yes, mamma. (*Stands back of table L.C.*)

DUCHESS OF BERWICK. Come and bid good-bye to Lady Windermere, and thank her for your charming visit. (*Coming down again.*) And by the way, I must thank you for sending a card to Mr. Hopper—he's that rich young Australian people are taking such notice of just at present. His father made a great fortune by selling some kind of food in circular tins—most palatable, I believe—I fancy it is the thing the servants always refuse to eat. But the son is quite interesting. I think he's attracted by dear Agatha's clever talk. Of course, we should be very sorry to lose her, but I think that a mother who doesn't part with a daughter every season has no real affection. We're coming to-night, dear. (PARKER *opens C. doors.*) And remember my advice, take the poor fellow out of town at once, it is the only thing to do. Good-bye, once more; come, Agatha.

Exeunt DUCHESS *and* LADY AGATHA *C.*

LADY WINDERMERE. How horrible! I understand now what Lord Darlington meant by the imaginary instance of the couple not two years married. Oh! it can't be true—she spoke of enormous sums of money paid to this woman. I know where Arthur keeps his bank book—in one of the drawers of that desk. I might find out by that. I *will* find out. (*Opens drawer.*) No, it is some hideous mistake. (*Rises and goes C.*) Some silly scandal! He loves *me*! He loves *me*! But why should I not look? I am his wife, I have a right to look! (*Returns to bureau, takes out book and examines it page by page, smiles and gives a sigh of relief.*) I knew it! there is not a word of truth in this stupid story. (*Puts book back in drawer. As she does so, starts and takes out another book.*) A second book—private—locked! (*Tries to open it, but fails. Sees paper knife on bureau, and with it cuts cover from book. Begins to start at the first page.*) 'Mrs. Erlynne—£600—Mrs. Erlynne —£700—Mrs. Erlynne—£400.' Oh! it is true! It is true! How horrible! (*Throws book on floor.*)

Enter LORD WINDERMERE *C.*

LORD WINDERMERE. Well, dear, has the fan been sent home yet? (*Going R.C. Sees book.*) Margaret, you have cut open my bank book. You have no right to do such a thing!

LADY WINDERMERE. You think it wrong that you are found out, don't you?

LORD WINDERMERE. I think it wrong that a wife should spy on her husband.

LADY WINDERMERE..I did not spy on you. I never knew of this woman's existence till half an hour ago. Some one who pitied me was kind enough to tell me what every one in London knows already—your daily visits to Curzon Street, your mad infatuation, the monstrous sums of money you squander on this infamous woman! (*Crossing L.*)

LORD WINDERMERE. Margaret! don't talk like that of Mrs. Erlynne, you don't know how unjust it is!

LADY WINDERMERE (*turning to him*). You are very jealous of Mrs. Erlynne's honour. I wish you had been as jealous of mine.

LORD WINDERMERE. Your honour is untouched, Margaret. You don't think for a moment that—— (*Puts book back into desk.*)

LADY WINDERMERE. I think that you spend your money strangely. That is all. Oh, don't imagine I mind about the money. As far as I am concerned, you may squander everything we have. But what I *do* mind is that you who have loved me, you who have taught me to love you, should pass from the love that is given to the love that is bought. Oh, it's horrible! (*Sits on sofa.*) And it is I who feel degraded! *you* don't feel anything. I feel stained, utterly stained. You can't realise how hideous the last six months seems to me now—every kiss you have given me is tainted in my memory.

LORD WINDERMERE (*crossing to her*). Don't say that, Margaret. I never loved any one in the whole world but you.

LADY WINDERMERE (*rises*). Who is this woman, then? Why do you take a house for her?

LORD WINDERMERE. I did not take a house for her.

LADY WINDERMERE. You gave her the money to do it, which is the same thing.

LORD WINDERMERE. Margaret, as far as I have known Mrs. Erlynne——

LADY WINDERMERE. Is there a Mr. Erlynne—or is he a myth?

LORD WINDERMERE. Her husband died many years ago. She is alone in the world.

LADY WINDERMERE. No relations?

    A pause.

LORD WINDERMERE. None.

LADY WINDERMERE. Rather curious, isn't it? (*L.*)

LORD WINDERMERE (*L.C.*). Margaret, I was saying to you—and I beg you to listen to me—that as far as I have known Mrs. Erlynne, she has conducted herself well. If years ago——

LADY WINDERMERE. Oh! (*Crossing R.C.*) I don't want details about her life!

LORD WINDERMERE (*C.*). I am not going to give you any details about her life. I tell you simply this—Mrs. Erlynne was once honoured, loved, respected. She was well born, she had position—she lost everything—threw it away, if you like. That makes it all the more bitter. Misfortunes one can endure—they come from outside, they are accidents. But to suffer for one's own faults—ah!—there is the sting of life. It was twenty years ago, too. She was little more than a girl then. She had been a wife for even less time than you have.

LADY WINDERMERE. I am not interested in her—and—you should not mention this woman and me in the same breath. It is an error of taste. (*Sitting R. at desk.*)

LORD WINDERMERE. Margaret, you could save this woman. She wants to get back into society, and she wants you to help her. (*Crossing to her.*)

LADY WINDERMERE. Me!

LORD WINDERMERE. Yes you.

LADY WINDERMERE. How impertinent of her!

A pause.

LORD WINDERMERE. Margaret, I came to ask you a great favour, and I still ask it of you, though you have discovered what I had intended you should never have known that I have given Mrs. Erlynne a large sum of money. I want you to send her an invitation for our party to-night. (*Standing L. of her.*)

LADY WINDERMERE. You are mad! (*Rises.*)

LORD WINDERMERE. I entreat you. People may chatter about her, do chatter about her, of course, but they don't know anything definite against her. She has been to several houses —not to houses where you would go, I admit, but still to houses where women who are in what is called Society nowadays do go. That does not content her. She wants you to receive her once.

LADY WINDERMERE. As a triumph for her, I suppose?

LORD WINDERMERE. No; but because she knows that you are a good woman—and that if she comes here once she will have a chance of a happier, a surer life than she has had. She will make no further effort to know you. Won't you help a woman who is trying to get back?

LADY WINDERMERE. No! If a woman really repents, she never wishes to return to the society that has made or seen her ruin.

LORD WINDERMERE. I beg of you.

LADY WINDERMERE (*crossing to door R.*). I am going to dress for dinner, and don't mention the subject again this evening. Arthur (*going to him C.*), you fancy because I have no father or mother that I am alone in the world, and that you can treat me as you choose. You are wrong, I have friends, many friends.

LORD WINDERMERE (*L.C.*). Margaret, you are talking foolishly, recklessly. I won't argue with you, but I insist upon your asking Mrs. Erlynne to-night.

LADY WINDERMERE (*R.C.*). I shall do nothing of the kind. (*Crossing L.C.*)

LORD WINDERMERE. You refuse? (*C.*)

LADY WINDERMERE. Absolutely!

LORD WINDERMERE. Ah, Margaret, do this for my sake; it is her last chance.

LADY WINDERMERE. What has that to do with me?

LORD WINDERMERE. How hard good women are!

LADY WINDERMERE. How weak bad men are!

LORD WINDERMERE. Margaret, none of us men may be good enough for the women we marry—that is quite true—but you don't imagine I would ever—oh, the suggestion is monstrous!

LADY WINDERMERE. Why should *you* be different from other men? I am told that there is hardly a husband in

London who does not waste his life over *some* shameful passion.

LORD WINDERMERE. I am not one of them.

LADY WINDERMERE. I am not sure of that!

LORD WINDERMERE. You are sure in your heart. But don't make chasm after chasm between us. God knows the last few minutes have thrust us wide enough apart. Sit down and write the card.

LADY WINDERMERE. Nothing in the whole world would induce me.

LORD WINDERMERE (*crossing to bureau*). Then I will! (*Rings electric bell, sits and writes card.*)

LADY WINDERMERE. You are going to invite this woman? (*Crossing to him.*)

LORD WINDERMERE. Yes.

Pause. Enter PARKER.

Parker!

PARKER. Yes, my lord. (*Comes down L.C.*)

LORD WINDERMERE. Have this note sent to Mrs. Erlynne at No. 84A Curzon Street. (*Crossing to L.C. and giving note to* PARKER.) There is no answer!

Exit PARKER *C.*

LADY WINDERMERE. Arthur, if that woman comes here, I shall insult her.

LORD WINDERMERE. Margaret, don't say that.

LADY WINDERMERE. I mean it.

LORD WINDERMERE. Child, if you did such a thing, there's not a woman in London who wouldn't pity you.

LADY WINDERMERE. There is not a *good* woman in London who would not applaud me. We have been too lax. We must make an example. I propose to begin to-night. (*Picking up fan.*) Yes, you gave me this fan to-day; it was your birthday present. If that woman crosses my threshold, I shall strike her across the face with it.

LORD WINDERMERE. Margaret, you couldn't do such a thing.

LADY WINDERMERE. You don't know me! (*Moves R.*)

Enter PARKER.

Parker!

PARKER. Yes, my lady.

LADY WINDERMERE. I shall dine in my own room. I don't want dinner, in fact. See that everything is ready by half-past ten. And, Parker, be sure you pronounce the names of the guests very distinctly to-night. Sometimes you speak so fast that I miss them. I am particularly anxious to hear the names quite clearly, so as to make no mistake. You understand, Parker?

PARKER. Yes, my lady.

LADY WINDERMERE. That will do!

Exit PARKER *C.*

(*Speaking to* LORD WINDERMERE.) Arthur, if that woman comes here—I warn you——

LORD WINDERMERE. Margaret, you'll ruin us!

LADY WINDERMERE. Us! From this moment my life is separate from yours. But if you wish to avoid a public scandal, write at once to this woman, and tell here that I forbid her to come here!

LORD WINDERMERE. I will not—I cannot—she must come!

LADY WINDERMERE. Then I shall do exactly as I have said. (*Goes R.*) You leave me no choice. (*Exit R.*)

LORD WINDERMERE (*calling after her*). Margaret! Margaret! (*A pause.*) My God! What shall I do? I dare not tell her who this woman really is. The shame would kill her. (*Sinks down into a chair and buries his face in his hands.*)

Curtain

Second Act

SCENE

Drawing-room in Lord Windermere's house. Door R.U. opening into ball-room, where band is playing. Door L. through which guests are entering. Door L.U. opens on to illuminated terrace. Palms, flowers, and brilliant lights. Room crowded with guests. Lady Windermere is receiving them.

DUCHESS OF BERWICK (*up C.*). So strange Lord Windermere isn't here. Mr. Hopper is very late, too. You have kept those five dances for him, Agatha? (*Comes down.*)

LADY AGATHA. Yes, mamma.

DUCHESS OF BERWICK (*sitting on sofa*). Just let me see your card. I'm so glad Lady Windermere has revived cards.— They're a mother's only safeguard. You dear simple little thing! (*Scratches out two names.*) No nice girl should ever waltz with such particularly younger sons! It looks so fast! The last two dances you might pass on the terrace with Mr. Hopper.

Enter MR. DUMBY *and* LADY PLYMDALE *from the ball-room.*

LADY AGATHA. Yes, mamma.

DUCHESS OF BERWICK (*fanning herself*). The air is so pleasant there.

PARKER. Mrs. Cowper-Cowper. Lady Stutfield. Sir James
Royston. Mr. Guy Berkeley.

These people enter as announced.

DUMBY. Good evening, Lady Stutfield. I suppose this will be
the last ball of the season?

LADY STUTFIELD. I suppose so, Mr. Dumby. It's been a
delightful season, hasn't it?

DUMBY. Quite delightful! Good evening, Duchess. I suppose
this will be the last ball of the season?

DUCHESS OF BERWICK. I suppose so, Mr. Dumby. It has
been a very dull season, hasn't it?

DUMBY. Dreadfully dull! Dreadfully dull!

MRS. COWPER-COWPER. Good evening, Mr. Dumby. I
suppose this will be the last ball of the season?

DUMBY. Oh, I think not. There'll probably be two more.
(*Wanders back to* LADY PLYMDALE.)

PARKER. Mr. Rufford. Lady Jedburgh and Miss Graham.
Mr. Hopper.

These people enter as announced.

HOPPER. How do you do, Lady Windermere? How do you
do, Duchess? (*Bows to* LADY AGATHA.)

DUCHESS OF BERWICK. Dear Mr. Hopper, how nice of you
to come so early. We all know how you are run after in
London.

HOPPER. Capital place, London! They are not nearly so
exclusive in London as they are in Sydney.

DUCHESS OF BERWICK. Ah! we know your value, Mr. Hopper. We wish there were more like you. It would make life
so much easier. Do you know, Mr. Hopper, dear Agatha
and I are so much interested in Australia. It must be so
pretty with all the dear little kangaroos flying about. Agatha
has found it on the map. What a curious shape it is! Just

like a large packing case. However, it is a very young country, isn't it?

HOPPER. Wasn't it made at the same time as the others, Duchess?

DUCHESS OF BERWICK. How clever you are, Mr. Hopper. You have a cleverness quite of your own. Now I mustn't keep you.

HOPPER. But I should like to dance with Lady Agatha, Duchess.

DUCHESS OF BERWICK. Well, I *hope* she has a dance left. Have you a dance left, Agatha?

LADY AGATHA. Yes, mamma.

DUCHESS OF BERWICK. The next one?

LADY AGATHA. Yes, mamma.

HOPPER. May I have the pleasure? (LADY AGATHA *bows*.)

DUCHESS OF BERWICK. Mind you take great care of my little chatterbox, Mr. Hopper.

LADY AGATHA *and* MR. HOPPER *pass into ball-room.*

Enter LORD WINDERMERE *L.*

LORD WINDERMERE. Margaret, I want to speak to you.

LADY WINDERMERE. In a moment.

The music stops.

PARKER. Lord Augustus Lorton.

Enter LORD AUGUSTUS.

LORD AUGUSTUS. Good evening, Lady Windermere.

DUCHESS OF BERWICK. Sir James, will you take me into the ball-room? Augustus has been dining with us to-night. I really have had quite enough of dear Augustus for the moment.

SIR JAMES ROYSTON *gives the* DUCHESS *his arm and escorts her into the ball-room.*

PARKER. Mr. and Mrs. Arthur Bowden. Lord and Lady Paisley. Lord Darlington.

These people enter as announced.

LORD AUGUSTUS (*coming up to* LORD WINDERMERE). Want to speak to you particularly, dear boy. I'm worn to a shadow. Know I don't look it. None of us men do look what we really are. Demmed good thing, too. What I want to know is this. Who is she? Where does she come from? Why hasn't she got any demmed relations? Demmed nuisance, relations! But they make one so demmed respectable.

LORD WINDERMERE. You are talking of Mrs. Erlynne, I suppose? I only met her six months ago. Till then, I never knew of her existence.

LORD AUGUSTUS. You have seen a good deal of her since then.

LORD WINDERMERE (*coldly*). Yes, I have seen a good deal of her since then. I have just seen her.

LORD AUGUSTUS. Egad! the women are very down on her. I have been dining with Arabella this evening! By Jove! you should have heard what she said about Mrs. Erlynne. She didn't leave a rag on her. . . . (*Aside.*) Berwick and I told her that didn't matter much, as the lady in question must have an extremely fine figure. You should have seen Arabella's expression! . . . But, look here, dear boy. I don't know what to do about Mrs. Erlynne. Egad! I might be married to her; she treats me with such demmed indifference. She's deuced clever, too! She explains everything. Egad! she explains you. She has got any amount of explanations for you—and all of them different.

LORD WINDERMERE. No explanations are necessary about my friendship with Mrs. Erlynne.

LORD AUGUSTUS. Hem! Well, look here, dear old fellow. Do you think she will ever get into this demmed thing called

Society? Would you introduce her to your wife? No use beating about the confounded bush. Would you do that?

LORD WINDERMERE. Mrs. Erlynne is coming here to-night.

LORD AUGUSTUS. Your wife has sent her a card?

LORD WINDERMERE. Mrs. Erlynne has received a card.

LORD AUGUSTUS. Then she's all right, dear boy. But why didn't you tell me that before? It would have saved me a heap of worry and demmed misunderstandings!

LADY AGATHA and MR. HOPPER cross and exit on terrace L.U.E.

PARKER. Mr. Cecil Graham!

Enter MR. CECIL GRAHAM.

CECIL GRAHAM (*bows to* LADY WINDERMERE, *passes over and shakes hands with* LORD WINDERMERE). Good evening, Arthur. Why don't you ask me how I am? I like people to ask me how I am. It shows a wide-spread interest in my health. Now, to-night I am not at all well. Been dining with my people. Wonder why it is one's people are always so tedious? My father would talk morality after dinner. I told him he was old enough to know better. But my experience is that as soon as people are old enough to know better, they don't know anything at all. Hallo, Tuppy! Hear you're going to be married again; thought you were tired of that game.

LORD AUGUSTUS. You're excessively trivial, my dear boy, excessively trivial!

CECIL GRAHAM. By the way, Tuppy, which is it? Have you been twice married and once divorced, or twice·divorced and once married? I say you've been twice divorced and once married. It seems so much more probable.

LORD AUGUSTUS. I have a very bad memory. I really don't remember which. (*Moves away R.*)

LADY PLYMDALE. Lord Windermere, I've something most particular to ask you.

LORD WINDERMERE. I am afraid—if you will excuse me—I must join my wife.

LADY PLYMDALE. Oh, you mustn't dream of such a thing. It's most dangerous nowadays for a husband to pay any attention to his wife in public. It always makes people think that he beats her when they're alone. The world has grown so suspicious of anything that looks like a happy married life. But I'll tell you what it is at supper. (*Moves towards door of ball-room.*)

LORD WINDERMERE (*C.*). Margaret! I *must* speak to you.

LADY WINDERMERE. Will you hold my fan for me, Lord Darlington? Thanks. (*Comes down to him.*)

LORD WINDERMERE (*crossing to her*). Margaret, what you said before dinner was, of course, impossible?

LADY WINDERMERE. That woman is not coming here to-night!

LORD WINDERMERE (*R.C.*). Mrs. Erlynne is coming here, and if you in any way annoy or wound her, you will bring shame and sorrow on us both. Remember that! Ah, Margaret! only trust me! A wife should trust her husband!

LADY WINDERMERE (*C.*). London is full of women who trust their husbands. One can always recognise them. They look so thoroughly unhappy. I am not going to be one of them. (*Moves up.*) Lord Darlington, will you give me back my fan, please? Thanks. . . . A useful thing a fan, isn't it? . . . I want a friend to-night, Lord Darlington: I didn't know I would want one so soon.

LORD DARLINGTON. Lady Windermere! I knew the time would come some day; but why to-night?

LORD WINDERMERE. I *will* tell her. I must. It would be terrible if there were any scene. Margaret . . .

PARKER. Mrs. Erlynne!

> LORD WINDERMERE *starts.* MRS. ERLYNNE *enters very beautifully dressed and very dignified.* LADY WINDERMERE *clutches at her fan, then lets it drop on the floor. She bows coldly to* MRS. ERLYNNE, *who bows to her sweetly in turn, and sails into the room.*

LORD DARLINGTON. You have dropped your fan, Lady Windermere. (*Picks it up and hands it to her.*)

MRS ERLYNNE (*C.*). How do you do, again, Lord Windermere? How charming your sweet wife looks! Quite a picture!

LORD WINDERMERE (*in a low voice*). It was terribly rash of you to come!

MRS. ERLYNNE (*smiling*). The wisest thing I ever did in my life. And, by the way, you must pay me a good deal of attention this evening. I am afraid of the women. You must introduce me to some of them. The men I can always manage. How do you do, Lord Augustus? You have quite neglected me lately. I have not seen you since yesterday. I am afraid you're faithless. Every one told me so.

LORD AUGUSTUS (*R.*). Now really, Mrs. Erlynne, allow me to explain.

MRS. ERLYNNE (*R.C.*). No, dear Lord Augustus, you can't explain anything. It is your chief charm.

LORD AUGUSTUS. Ah! if you find charms in me, Mrs. Erlynne——

> *They converse together.* LORD WINDERMERE *moves uneasily about the room watching* MRS. ERLYNNE.

LORD DARLINGTON (*to* LADY WINDERMERE). How pale you are!

LADY WINDERMERE. Cowards are always pale!

LORD DARLINGTON. You look faint. Come out on the terrace.

LADY WINDERMERE. Yes. (*To* PARKER.) Parker, send my cloak out.

MRS. ERLYNNE (*crossing to her*). Lady Windermere, how beautifully your terrace is illuminated. Reminds me of Prince Doria's at Rome.

> LADY WINDERMERE *bows coldly, and goes off with* LORD DARLINGTON.

Oh, how do you do, Mr. Graham? Isn't that your aunt, Lady Jedburgh? I should so much like to know her.

CECIL GRAHAM (*after a moment's hesitation and embarrassment*). Oh, certainly, if you wish it. Aunt Caroline, allow me to introduce Mrs. Erlynne.

MRS. ERLYNNE. So pleased to meet you, Lady Jedburgh. (*Sits beside her on the sofa.*) Your nephew and I are great friends. I am so much interested in his political career. I think he's sure to be a wonderful success. He thinks like a Tory, and talks like a Radical, and that's so important nowadays. He's such a brilliant talker, too. But we all know from whom he inherits that. Lord Allandale was saying to me only yesterday, in the Park, that Mr. Graham talks almost as well as his aunt.

LADY JEDBURGH (*R.*). Most kind of you to say these charming things to me!

> MRS. ERLYNNE *smiles, and continues conversation.*

DUMBY (*to* CECIL GRAHAM). Did you introduce Mrs. Erlynne to Lady Jedburgh?

CECIL GRAHAM. Had to, my dear fellow. Couldn't help it! That woman can make one do anything she wants. How, I don't know.

DUMBY. Hope to goodness she won't speak to me! (*Saunters towards* LADY PLYMDALE.)

MRS. ERLYNNE (*C. to* LADY JEDBURGH). On Thursday? With great pleasure. (*Rises, and speaks to* LORD WINDERMERE, *laughing*.) What a bore it is to have to be civil to these old dowagers! But they always insist on it!

LADY PLYMDALE (*to* MR. DUMBY). Who is that well-dressed woman talking to Windermere?

DUMBY. Haven't got the slightest idea! Looks like an *édition de luxe* of a wicked French novel, meant specially for the English market.

MRS. ERLYNNE. So that is poor Dumby with Lady Plymdale? I hear she is frightfully jealous of him. He doesn't seem anxious to speak to me to-night. I suppose he is afraid of her. Those straw-coloured women have dreadful tempers. Do you know, I think I'll dance with you first, Windermere. (LORD WINDERMERE *bites his lip and frowns*.) It will make Lord Augustus so jealous! Lord Augustus! (LORD AUGUSTUS *comes down*.) Lord Windermere insists on my dancing with him first, and, as it's his own house, I can't well refuse. You know I would much sooner dance with you.

LORD AUGUSTUS (*with a low bow*). I wish I could think so, Mrs. Erlynne.

MRS. ERLYNNE. You know it far too well. I can fancy a person dancing through life with you and finding it charming.

LORD AUGUSTUS (*placing his hand on his white waistcoat*). Oh, thank you, thank you. You are the most adorable of all ladies!

MRS. ERLYNNE. What a nice speech! So simple and so sincere! Just the sort of speech I like. Well, you shall hold my bouquet. (*Goes towards ball-room on* LORD WINDERMERE'S *arm*.) Ah, Mr. Dumby, how are you? I am so sorry I have been out the last three times you have called. Come and lunch on Friday.

DUMBY (*with perfect nonchalance*). Delighted!

> LADY PLYMDALE *glares with indignation at* MR. DUMBY. LORD AUGUSTUS *follows* MRS. ERLYNNE *and* LORD WINDERMERE *into the ball-room holding bouquet*.

LADY PLYMDALE (*to* MR. DUMBY). What an absolute brute you are! I never can believe a word you say! Why did you tell me you didn't know her? What do you mean by calling on her three times running? You are not to go to lunch there; of course you understand that?

DUMBY. My dear Laura, I wouldn't dream of going!

LADY PLYMDALE. You haven't told me her name yet! Who is she?

DUMBY (*coughs slightly and smooths his hair*). She's a Mrs. Erlynne.

LADY PLYMDALE. That woman!

DUMBY. Yes; that is what every one calls her.

LADY PLYMDALE. How very interesting! How intensely interesting! I really must have a good stare at her. (*Goes to door of ball-room and looks in.*) I have heard the most shocking things about her. They say she is ruining poor Windermere. And Lady Windermere, who goes in for being so proper, invites her! How extremely amusing! It takes a thoroughly good woman to do a thoroughly stupid thing. You are to lunch there on Friday!

DUMBY. Why?

LADY PLYMDALE. Because I want you to take my husband with you. He has been so attentive lately, that he has become a perfect nuisance. Now, this woman is just the thing for him. He'll dance attendance upon her as long as she lets him, and won't bother me. I assure you, women of that kind are most useful. They form the basis of other people's marriages.

DUMBY. What a mystery you are!

LADY PLYMDALE (*looking at him*). I wish *you* were!

DUMBY. I am—to myself. I am the only person in the world I should like to know thoroughly; but I don't see any chance of it just at present.

They pass into the ball-room, and LADY WINDERMERE *and* LORD DARLINGTON *enter from the terrace.*

LADY WINDERMERE. Yes. Her coming here is monstrous, unbearable. I know now what you meant to-day at tea time. Why didn't you tell me right out? You should have!

LORD DARLINGTON. I couldn't! A man can't tell these things about another man! But if I had known he was going to make you ask her here to-night, I think I would have told you. That insult, at any rate, you would have been spared.

LADY WINDERMERE. I did not ask her. He insisted on her coming—against my entreaties—against my commands. Oh! the house is tainted for me! I feel that every woman here sneers at me as she dances by with my husband. What have I done to deserve this? I gave him all my life. He took it—used it—spoiled it! I am degraded in my own eyes; and I lack courage—I am a coward! (*Sits down on sofa.*)

LORD DARLINGTON. If I know you at all, I know that you can't live with a man who treats you like this! What sort of life would you have with him? You would feel that he was lying to you every moment of the day. You would feel that the look in his eyes was false, his voice false, his touch false, his passion false. He would come to you when he was weary of others; you would have to comfort him. He would come to you when he was devoted to others; you would have to charm him. You would have to be to him the mask of his real life, the cloak to hide his secret.

LADY WINDERMERE. You are right—you are terribly right. But where am I to turn? You said you would be my friend, Lord Darlington.—Tell me, what am I to do? Be my friend now.

LORD DARLINGTON. Between men and women there is no friendship possible. There is passion, enmity, worship, love, but no friendship. I love you——

LADY WINDERMERE. No, no! (*Rises.*)

LORD DARLINGTON. Yes, I love you! You are more to me than anything in the whole world. What does your husband give you? Nothing. Whatever is in him he gives to this wretched woman, whom he has thrust into your society, into your home, to shame you before every one. I offer you my life——

LADY WINDERMERE. Lord Darlington!

LORD DARLINGTON. My life—my whole life. Take it, and do with it what you will. . . . I love you—love you as I have never loved any living thing. From the moment I met you I loved you, loved you blindly, adoringly, madly! You did not know it then—you know it now! Leave this house to-night. I won't tell you that the world matters nothing, or the world's voice, or the voice of society. They matter a great deal. They matter far too much. But there are moments when one has to choose between living one's own life, fully, entirely, completely—or dragging out some false, shallow, degrading existence that the world in its hypocrisy demands. You have that moment now. Choose! Oh, my love, choose.

LADY WINDERMERE (*moving slowly away from him, and looking at him with startled eyes*). I have not the courage.

LORD DARLINGTON (*following her*). Yes; you have the courage. There may be six months of pain, of disgrace even, but when you no longer bear his name, when you bear mine, all will be well. Margaret, my love, my wife that shall be some day—yes, my wife! You know it! What are you now? This woman has the place that belongs by right to you. Oh! go—go out of this house, with head erect, with a smile upon your lips, with courage in your eyes. All London will know why you did it; and who will blame you? No one. If they do, what matter? Wrong? What is wrong? It's wrong for a man to abandon his wife for a shameless woman. It is wrong for a wife to remain with a man who so dishonours her. You said once you would make no compromise with things. Make none now. Be brave! Be yourself!

LADY WINDERMERE. I am afraid of being myself. Let me think! Let me wait! My husband may return to me. (*Sits down on sofa.*)

LORD DARLINGTON. And you would take him back! You are not what I thought you were. You are just the same as every other woman. You would stand anything rather than face the censure of a world, whose praise you would despise. In a week you will be driving with this woman in the Park. She will be your constant guest—your dearest friend. You would endure anything rather than break with one blow this monstrous tie. You are right. You have no courage; none!

LADY WINDERMERE. Ah, give me time to think. I cannot answer you now. (*Passes her hand nervously over her brow.*)

LORD DARLINGTON. It must be now or not at all.

LADY WINDERMERE (*rising from the sofa*). Then, not at all!

A pause.

LORD DARLINGTON. You break my heart!

LADY WINDERMERE. Mine is already broken.

A pause.

LORD DARLINGTON. To-morrow I leave England. This is the last time I shall ever look on you. You will never see me again. For one moment our lives met—our souls touched. They must never meet or touch again. Good-bye, Margaret. (*Exit.*)

LADY WINDERMERE. How alone I am in life! How terribly alone!

The music stops. Enter the DUCHESS OF BERWICK *and* LORD PAISLEY *laughing and talking. Other guests come on from ball-room.*

DUCHESS OF BERWICK. Dear Margaret, I've just been having such a delightful chat with Mrs. Erlynne. I am so sorry for what I said to you this afternoon about her. Of course, she must be all right if *you* invite her. A most attractive woman, and has such sensible views on life. Told me she entirely disapproved of people marrying more than once, so I feel quite safe about poor Augustus. Can't imagine why people speak against her. It's those horrid nieces of mine—the Saville girls—they're always talking scandal. Still, I should go to Homburg, dear, I really should. She is just a little too attractive. But where is Agatha? Oh, there she is. (LADY AGATHA *and* MR. HOPPER *enter from terrace L.U. E.*) Mr. Hopper, I am very, very angry with you. You have taken Agatha out on the terrace, and she is so delicate.

HOPPER (*L.C.*). Awfully sorry, Duchess. We went out for a moment and then got chatting together.

DUCHESS OF BERWICK (*C.*). Ah, about dear Australia, I suppose?

HOPPER. Yes!

DUCHESS OF BERWICK. Agatha, darling! (*Beckons her over.*)

LADY AGATHA. Yes, mamma!

DUCHESS OF BERWICK (*aside*). Did Mr. Hopper definitely——

LADY AGATHA. Yes, mamma.

DUCHESS OF BERWICK. And what answer did you give him, dear child?

LADY AGATHA. Yes, mamma.

DUCHESS OF BERWICK (*affectionately*). My dear one! You always say the right thing. Mr. Hopper! James! Agatha has told me everything. How cleverly you have both kept your secret.

HOPPER. You don't mind my taking Agatha off to Australia, then, Duchess?

DUCHESS OF BERWICK (*indignantly*). To Australia? Oh, don't mention that dreadful vulgar place.

HOPPER. But she said she'd like to come with me.

DUCHESS OF BERWICK (*severely*). Did you say that, Agatha?

LADY AGATHA. Yes, mamma.

DUCHESS OF BERWICK. Agatha, you say the most silly things possible. I think on the whole that Grosvenor Square would be a more healthy place to reside in. There are lots of vulgar people live in Grosvenor Square, but at any rate there are no horrid kangaroos crawling about. But we'll talk about that to-morrow. James, you can take Agatha down. You'll come to lunch, of course, James. At half-past one, instead of two. The Duke will wish to say a few words to you, I am sure.

HOPPER. I should like to have a chat with the Duke, Duchess. He has not said a single word to me yet.

DUCHESS OF BERWICK. I think you'll find he will have a great deal to say to you to-morrow. (*Exit* LADY AGATHA *with* MR. HOPPER.) And now good-night, Margaret. I'm afraid it's the old, old story, dear. Love—well, not love at first sight, but love at the end of the season, which is so much more satisfactory.

LADY WINDERMERE. Good-night, Duchess.

Exit the DUCHESS OF BERWICK *on* LORD PAISLEY'S *arm.*

LADY PLYMDALE. My dear Margaret, what a handsome woman your husband has been dancing with! I should be quite jealous if I were you! Is she a great friend of yours?

LADY WINDERMERE. No!

LADY PLYMDALE. Really? Good-night, dear. (*Looks at* MR. DUMBY *and exit.*)

DUMBY. Awful manners young Hopper has!

CECIL GRAHAM. Ah! Hopper is one of Nature's gentlemen, the worst type of gentleman I know.

DUMBY. Sensible woman, Lady Windermere. Lots of wives
would have objected to Mrs. Erlynne coming. But Lady
Windermere has that uncommon thing called common
sense.

CECIL GRAHAM. And Windermere knows that nothing looks
so like innocence as an indiscretion.

DUMBY. Yes; dear Windermere is becoming almost modern.
Never thought he would. (*Bows to* LADY WINDERMERE
and exit.)

LADY JEDBURGH. Good-night, Lady Windermere. What a
fascinating woman Mrs. Erlynne is! She is coming to lunch
on Thursday, won't you come too? I expect the Bishop and
dear Lady Merton.

LADY WINDERMERE. I am afraid I am engaged, Lady Jedburgh.

LADY JEDBURGH. So sorry. Come, dear. (*Exeunt* LADY JED-
BURGH *and* MISS GRAHAM.)

Enter MRS. ERLYNNE *and* LORD WINDERMERE.

MRS. ERLYNNE. Charming ball it has been! Quite reminds
me of old days. (*Sits on sofa.*) And I see that there are just
as many fools in society as there used to be. So pleased to
find that nothing has altered! Except Margaret. She's grown
quite pretty. The last time I saw her—twenty years ago,
she was a fright in flannel. Positive fright, I assure you. The
dear Duchess! and that sweet Lady Agatha! Just the type of
girl I like! Well, really, Windermere, if I am to be the
Duchess's sister-in-law——

LORD WINDERMERE (*sitting L. of her*). But are you——?

Exit MR. CECIL GRAHAM *with rest of guests.* LADY
WINDERMERE *watches, with a look of scorn and pain,*
MRS. ERLYNNE *and her husband. They are unconscious of
her presence.*

MRS. ERLYNNE. Oh, yes! He's to call to-morrow at twelve o'clock! He wanted to propose to-night. In fact he did. He kept on proposing. Poor Augustus, you know how he repeats himself. Such a bad habit! But I told him I wouldn't give him an answer till to-morrow. Of course I am going to take him. And I dare say I'll make him an admirable wife, as wives go. And there is a great deal of good in Lord Augustus. Fortunately it is all on the surface. Just where good qualities should be. Of course you must help me in this matter.

LORD WINDERMERE. I am not called on to encourage Lord Augustus, I suppose?

MRS. ERLYNNE. Oh, no! I do the encouraging. But you will make me a handsome settlement, Windermere, won't you?

LORD WINDERMERE (*frowning*). Is that what you want to talk to me about to-night?

MRS. ERLYNNE. Yes.

LORD WINDERMERE (*with a gesture of impatience*). I will not talk of it here.

MRS. ERLYNNE (*laughing*). Then we will talk of it on the terrace. Even business should have a picturesque background. Should it not, Windermere? With a proper background women can do anything.

LORD WINDERMERE. Won't to-morrow do as well?

MRS. ERLYNNE. No; you see, to-morrow I am going to accept him. And I think it would be a good thing if I was able to tell him that I had—well, what shall I say?— £2000 a year left to me by a third cousin—or a second husband—or some distant relative of that kind. It would be an additional attraction, wouldn't it? You have a delightful opportunity now of paying me a compliment, Windermere. But you are not very clever at paying compliments. I am afraid Margaret doesn't encourage you in that excellent habit. It's a great mistake on her part. When men give up saying what is charming, they give up thinking what is

charming. But seriously, what do you say to £2000? £2500,
I think. In modern life margin is everything. Windermere,
don't you think the world an intensely amusing place?
I do!

Exit on terrace with LORD WINDERMERE. *Music strikes
up in ball-room.*

LADY WINDERMERE. To stay in this house any longer is impossible. To-night a man who loves me offered me his
whole life. I refused it. It was foolish of me. I will offer him
mine now. I will give him mine. I will go to him! (*Puts on
cloak and goes to the door, then turns back. Sits down at table
and writes a letter, puts it into an envelope, and leaves it on
table.*) Arthur has never understood me. When he reads
this, he will. He may do as he chooses now with his life. I
have done with mine as I think best, as I think right. It is
he who has broken the bond of marriage—not I. I only
break its bondage.

Exit.

PARKER *enters L. and crosses towards the ball-room R.
Enter* MRS. ERLYNNE.

MRS. ERLYNNE. Is Lady Windermere in the ball-room?
PARKER. Her ladyship has just gone out.
MRS. ERLYNNE. Gone out? She's not on the terrace?
PARKER. No, madam. Her ladyship has just gone out of the
house.
MRS. ERLYNNE (*starts, and looks at the servant with a puzzled
expression in her face*). Out of the house?
PARKER. Yes, madam—her ladyship told me she had left a
letter for his lordship on the table.
MRS. ERLYNNE. A letter for Lord Windermere?
PARKER. Yes, madam.
MRS. ERLYNNE. Thank you.

Exit PARKER. *The music in the ball-room stops.*

Gone out of her house! A letter addressed to her husband! (*Goes over to bureau and looks at letter. Takes it up and lays it down again with a shudder of fear.*) No, no! It would be impossible! Life doesn't repeat its tragedies like that! Oh, why does this horrible fancy come across me? Why do I remember now the one moment of my life I most wish to forget? Does life repeat its tragedies? (*Tears letter open and reads it, then sinks down into a chair with a gesture of anguish.*) Oh, how terrible! The same words that twenty years ago I wrote to her father! and how bitterly I have been punished for it! No; my punishment, my real punishment is to-night, is now! (*Still seated R.*)

Enter LORD WINDERMERE *L.U.E.*

LORD WINDERMERE. Have you said good-night to my wife? (*Comes C.*)

MRS. ERLYNNE (*crushing letter in her hand*). Yes.

LORD WINDERMERE. Where is she?

MRS. ERLYNNE. She is very tired. She has gone to bed. She said she had a headache.

LORD WINDERMERE. I must go to her. You'll excuse me?

MRS. ERLYNNE (*rising hurriedly*). Oh, no! It's nothing serious. She's only very tired, that is all. Besides, there are people still in the supper-room. She wants you to make her apologies to them. She said she didn't wish to be disturbed. (*Drops letter.*) She asked me to tell you!

LORD WINDERMERE (*picks up letter*). You have dropped something.

MRS. ERLYNNE. Oh yes, thank you, that is mine. (*Puts out her hand to take it.*)

LORD WINDERMERE (*still looking at letter*). But it's my wife's hand-writing, isn't it?

MRS. ERLYNNE (*takes the letter quickly*). Yes, it's—an address. Will you ask them to call my carriage, please?

LORD WINDERMERE. Certainly. (*Goes L. and Exit.*)

MRS. ERLYNNE. Thanks! What can I do? What can I do? I feel a passion awakening within me that I never felt before. What can it mean? The daughter must not be like the mother—that would be terrible. How can I save her? How can I save my child? A moment may ruin a life. Who knows that better than I? Windermere must be got out of the house; that is absolutely necessary. (*Goes L.*) But how shall I do it? It must be done somehow. Ah!

Enter LORD AUGUSTUS *R.U.E. carrying bouquet.*

LORD AUGUSTUS. Dear lady, I am in such suspense! May I not have an answer to my request?

MRS. ERLYNNE. Lord Augustus, listen to me. You are to take Lord Windermere down to your club at once, and keep him there as long as possible. You understand?

LORD AUGUSTUS. But you said you wished me to keep early hours!

MRS. ERLYNNE (*nervously*). Do what I tell you. Do what I tell you.

LORD AUGUSTUS. And my reward?

MRS. ERLYNNE. Your reward? Your reward? Oh, ask me that to-morrow. But don't let Windermere out of your sight to-night. If you do I will never forgive you. I will never speak to you again. I'll have nothing to do with you. Remember you are to keep Windermere at your club, and don't let him come back to-night. (*Exit. L.*)

LORD AUGUSTUS. Well, really, I might be her husband already. Positively I might. (*Follows her in a bewildered manner.*)

Curtain

Third Act

SCENE

*Lord Darlington's Rooms. A large sofa is in front of fireplace R.
At the back of the stage a curtain is drawn across the window.
Doors L. and R. Table R. with writing materials. Table C. with
syphons, glasses, and Tantalus frame. Table L. with cigar and
cigarette box. Lamps lit.*

LADY WINDERMERE (*standing by the fireplace*). Why doesn't
he come? This waiting is horrible. He should be here. Why
is he not here, to wake by passionate words some fire within
me? I am cold—cold as a loveless thing. Arthur must have
read my letter by this time. If he cared for me, he would
have come after me, would have taken me back by force.
But he doesn't care. He's entrammelled by this woman—
fascinated by her—dominated by her. If a woman wants to
hold a man, she has merely to appeal to what is worst in
him. We make gods of men and they leave us. Others make
brutes of them and they fawn and are faithful. How hideous
life is! . . . Oh! it was mad of me to come here, horribly mad.
And yet, which is the worst, I wonder, to be at the mercy
of a man who loves one, or the wife of a man who in one's
own house dishonours one? What woman knows? What
woman in the whole world? But will he love me always, this
man to whom I am giving my life? What do I bring him?

Lips that have lost the note of joy, eyes that are blinded by tears, chill hands and icy heart. I bring him nothing. I must go back—no; I can't go back, my letter has put me in their power—Arthur would not take me back! That fatal letter! No! Lord Darlington leaves England to-morrow. I will go with him—I have no choice. (*Sits down for a few moments. Then starts up and puts on her cloak.*) No. no! I will go back, let Arthur do with me what he pleases. I can't wait here. It has been madness my coming. I must go at once. As for Lord Darlington—Oh! here he is! What shall I do? What can I say to him? Will he let me go away at all? I have heard that men are brutal, horrible . . . Oh! (*Hides her face in her hands.*)

Enter MRS. ERLYNNE *L.*

MRS. ERLYNNE. Lady Windermere! (LADY WINDERMERE *starts and looks up. Then recoils in contempt.*) Thank Heaven I am in time. You must go back to your husband's house immediately.

LADY WINDERMERE. Must?

MRS. ERLYNNE (*authoritatively*). Yes, you must! There is not a second to be lost. Lord Darlington may return at any moment.

LADY WINDERMERE. Don't come near me!

MRS. ERLYNNE. Oh! You are on the brink of ruin, you are on the brink of a hideous precipice. You must leave this place at once, my carriage is waiting at the corner of the street. You must come with me and drive straight home.

LADY WINDERMERE *throws off her cloak and flings it on the sofa.*

What are you doing?

LADY WINDERMERE. Mrs. Erlynne—if you had not come here, I would have gone back. But now that I see you, I feel that nothing in the whole world would induce me to live under the same roof as Lord Windermere. You fill me with horror. There is something about you that stirs the wildest —rage within me. And I know why you are here. My husband sent you to lure me back that I might serve as a blind to whatever relations exist between you and him.

MRS. ERLYNNE. Oh! You don't think that—you can't.

LADY WINDERMERE. Go back to my husband, Mrs. Erlynne. He belongs to you and not to me. I suppose he is afraid of a scandal. Men are such cowards. They outrage every law of the world, and are afraid of the world's tongue. But he had better prepare himself. He shall have a scandal. He shall have the worst scandal there has been in London for years. He shall see his name in every vile paper, mine on every hideous placard.

MRS. ERLYNNE. No—no——

LADY WINDERMERE. Yes! he shall. Had he come himself, I admit I would have gone back to the life of degradation you and he had prepared for me—I was going back—but to stay himself at home, and to send you as his messenger—oh! it was infamous—infamous.

MRS. ERLYNNE (*C.*). Lady Windermere, you wrong me horribly—you wrong your husband horribly. He doesn't know you are here—he thinks you are safe in your own house. He thinks you are asleep in your own room. He never read the mad letter you wrote to him!

LADY WINDERMERE (*R.*). Never read it!

MRS. ERLYNNE. No—he knows nothing about it.

LADY WINDERMERE. How simple you think me! (*Going to her.*) You are lying to me!

MRS. ERLYNNE (*restraining herself*). I am not. I am telling you the truth.

LADY WINDERMERE. If my husband didn't read my letter, how is it that you are here? Who told you I had left the

house you were shameless enough to enter? Who told you
where I had gone to? My husband told you, and sent you
to decoy me back. (*Crosses L.*)

MRS. ERLYNNE (*R.C.*). Your husband has never seen the
letter. I—saw it, I opened it. I—read it.

LADY WINDERMERE (*turning to her*). You opened a letter of
mine to my husband? You wouldn't dare!

MRS. ERLYNNE. Dare! Oh! to save you from the abyss into
which you are falling, there is nothing in the world I would
not dare, nothing in the whole world. Here is the letter.
Your husband has never read it. He never shall read it.
(*Going to fireplace.*) It should never have been written.
(*Tears it and throws it into the fire.*)

LADY WINDERMERE (*with infinite contempt in her voice and
look*). How do I know that that was my letter after all? You
seem to think the commonest device can take me in!

MRS. ERLYNNE. Oh! why do you disbelieve everything I tell
you? What object do you think I have in coming here,
except to save you from utter ruin, to save you from the
consequence of a hideous mistake? That letter that is burnt
now *was* your letter. I swear it to you!

LADY WINDERMERE (*slowly*). You took good care to burn it
before I had examined it. I cannot trust you. You, whose
whole life is a lie, how could you speak the truth about
anything? (*Sits down.*)

MRS. ERLYNNE (*hurriedly*). Think as you like about me—
say what you choose against me, but go back, go back to the
husband you love.

LADY WINDERMERE (*sullenly*). I do *not* love him!

MRS. ERLYNNE. You do, and you know that he loves you.

LADY WINDERMERE. He does not understand what love is.
He understands it as little as you do—but I see what you
want. It would be a great advantage for you to get me back.
Dear Heaven! what a life I would have then! Living at the

mercy of a woman who has neither mercy nor pity in her, a woman whom it is an infamy to meet, a degradation to know, a vile woman, a woman who comes between husband and wife!

MRS. ERLYNNE (*with a gesture of despair*). Lady Windermere, Lady Windermere, don't say such terrible things. You don't know how terrible they are, how terrible and how unjust. Listen, you must listen! Only go back to your husband, and I promise you never to communicate with him again on any pretext—never to see him—never to have anything to do with his life or yours. The money that he gave me, he gave me not through love, but through hatred, not in worship, but in contempt. The hold I have over him——

LADY WINDERMERE (*rising*). Ah! you admit you have a hold!

MRS. ERLYNNE. Yes, and I will tell you what it is. It is his love for you, Lady Windermere.

LADY WINDERMERE. You expect me to believe that?

MRS. ERLYNNE. You must believe it! It is true. It is his love for you that has made him submit to—oh! call it what you like, tyranny, threats, anything you choose. But it is his love for you. His desire to spare you—shame, yes, shame and disgrace.

LADY WINDERMERE. What do you mean? You are insolent! What have I to do with you?

MRS. ERLYNNE (*humbly*). Nothing. I know it—but I tell you that your husband loves you—that you may never meet with such love again in your whole life—that such love you will never meet—and that if you throw it away, the day may come when you will starve for love and it will not be given to you, beg for love and it will be denied you—Oh! Arthur loves you!

LADY WINDERMERE. Arthur? And you tell me there is nothing between you?

MRS. ERLYNNE. Lady Windermere, before Heaven your
husband is guiltless of all offence towards you! And I—I
tell you that had it ever occurred to me that such a monstrous
suspicion would have entered your mind, I would have died
rather than have crossed your life or his—oh! died, gladly
died! (*Moves away to sofa R.*)

LADY WINDERMERE. You talk as if you had a heart. Women
like you have no hearts. Heart is not in you. You are bought
and sold. (*Sits L.C.*)

MRS. ERLYNNE (*starts, with a gesture of pain. Then restrains
herself, and comes over to where* LADY WINDERMERE *is
sitting. As she speaks, she stretches out her hands towards her,
but does not dare to touch her.*) Believe what you choose about
me. I am not worth a moment's sorrow. But don't spoil
your beautiful young life on my account! You don't know
what may be in store for you, unless you leave this house at
once. You don't know what it is to fall into the pit, to be
despised, mocked, abandoned, sneered at—to be an outcast!
to find the door shut against one, to have to creep in by
hideous byways, afraid every moment lest the mask should
be stripped from one's face, and all the while to hear the
laughter, the horrible laughter of the world, a thing more
tragic than all the tears the world has ever shed. You don't
know what it is. One pays for one's sin, and then one pays
again, and all one's life one pays. You must never know
that.—As for me, if suffering be an expiation, then at this
moment I have expiated all my faults, whatever they have
been; for to-night you have made a heart in one who had it
not, made it and broken it.—But let that pass. I may have
wrecked my own life, but I will not let you wreck yours. You
—why, you are a mere girl, you would be lost. You haven't
got the kind of brains that enables a woman to get back.
You have neither the wit nor the courage. You couldn't
stand dishonour! No! Go back, Lady Windermere, to the

husband who loves you, whom you love. You have a child, Lady Windermere. Go back to that child who even now, in pain or in joy, may be calling to you. LADY WINDERMERE *rises*.) God gave you that child. He will require from you that you make his life fine, that you watch over him. What answer will you make to God if his life is ruined through you? Back to your house, Lady Windermere—your husband loves you! He has never swerved for a moment from the love he bears you. But even if he had a thousand loves, you must stay with your child. If he was harsh to you, you must stay with your child. If he ill-treated you, you must stay with your child. If he abandoned you, your place is with your child.

LADY WINDERMERE *bursts into tears and buries her face in her hands.*

(*Rushing to her.*) Lady Windermere!

LADY WINDERMERE (*holding out her hands to her, helplessly, as a child might do*). Take me home. Take me home.

MRS. ERLYNNE (*is about to embrace her. Then restrains herself. There is a look of wonderful joy in her face.*) Come! Where is your cloak? (*Getting it from sofa.*) Here. Put it on. Come at once!

They go to the door.

LADY WINDERMERE. Stop! Don't you hear voices?

MRS. ERLYNNE. No, no! There is no one!

LADY WINDERMERE. Yes, there is! Listen! Oh! that is my husband's voice! He is coming in! Save me! Oh, it's some plot! You have sent for him.

Voices outside.

MRS. ERLYNNE. Silence! I'm here to save you, if I can. But I fear it is too late! There! (*Points to the curtain across the window.*) The first chance you have, slip out, if you ever get a chance!

LADY WINDERMERE. But you?

MRS. ERLYNNE. Oh! never mind me. I'll face them.

> LADY WINDERMERE *hides herself behind the curtain.*

LORD AUGUSTUS (*outside*). Nonsense, dear Windermere, you must not leave me!

MRS. ERLYNNE. Lord Augustus! Then it is I who am lost! (*Hesitates for a moment, then looks round and sees door R., and exit through it.*)

> *Enter* LORD DARLINGTON, MR. DUMBY, LORD WINDERMERE, LORD AUGUSTUS LORTON, *and* MR. CECIL GRAHAM.

DUMBY. What a nuisance their turning us out of the club at this hour! It's only two o'clock. (*Sinks into a chair.*) The lively part of the evening is only just beginning. (*Yawns and closes his eyes.*)

LORD WINDERMERE. It is very good of you, Lord Darlington, allowing Augustus to force our company on you, but I'm afraid I can't stay long.

LORD DARLINGTON. Really! I am so sorry! You'll take a cigar, won't you?

LORD WINDERMERE. Thanks! (*Sits down.*)

LORD AUGUSTUS (*to* LORD WINDERMERE). My dear boy, you must not dream of going. I have a great deal to talk to you about, of demmed importance, too. (*Sits down with him at L. table.*)

CECIL GRAHAM. Oh! We all know what that is! Tuppy can't talk about anything but Mrs. Erlynne.

LORD WINDERMERE. Well, that is no business of yours, is it, Cecil?

CECIL GRAHAM. None! That is why it interests me. My own business always bores me to death. I prefer other people's.

LORD DARLINGTON. Have something to drink, you fellows. Cecil, you'll have a whisky and soda?

CECIL GRAHAM. Thanks. (*Goes to table with* LORD DARLINGTON.) Mrs. Erlynne looked very handsome to-night, didn't she?

LORD DARLINGTON. I am not one of her admirers.

CECIL GRAHAM. I usen't to be, but I am now. Why! she actually made me introduce her to poor dear Aunt Caroline. I believe she is going to lunch there.

LORD DARLINGTON (*in surprise*). No?

CECIL GRAHAM. She is, really.

LORD DARLINGTON. Excuse me, you fellows. I'm going away to-morrow. And I have to write a few letters. (*Goes to writing table and sits down.*)

DUMBY. Clever woman, Mrs. Erlynne.

CECIL GRAHAM. Hallo, Dumby! I thought you were asleep.

DUMBY. I am, I usually am!

LORD AUGUSTUS. A very clever woman. Knows perfectly well what a demmed fool I am—knows it as well as I do myself.

CECIL GRAHAM *comes towards him laughing.*

Ah, you may laugh, my boy, but it is a great thing to come across a woman who thoroughly understands one.

DUMBY. It is an awfully dangerous thing. They always end by marrying one.

CECIL GRAHAM. But I thought, Tuppy, you were never going to see her again! Yes! you told me so yesterday evening at the club. You said you'd heard——

Whispering to him.

LORD AUGUSTUS. Oh, she's explained that.

CECIL GRAHAM. And the Wiesbaden affair?

LORD AUGUSTUS. She's explained that too.

DUMBY. And her income, Tuppy? Has she explained that?

LORD AUGUSTUS (*in a very serious voice*). She's going to explain that to-morrow.

   CECIL GRAHAM *goes back to C. table.*

DUMBY. Awfully commercial, women nowadays. Our grand-mothers threw their caps over the mills, of course, but, by Jove, their granddaughters only throw their caps over mills that can raise the wind for them.

LORD AUGUSTUS. You want to make her out a wicked woman. She is not!

CECIL GRAHAM. Oh! Wicked women bother one. Good women bore one. That is the only difference between them.

LORD AUGUSTUS (*puffing a cigar*). Mrs. Erlynne has a future before her.

DUMBY. Mrs. Erlynne has a past before her.

LORD AUGUSTUS. I prefer women with a past. They're always so demmed amusing to talk to.

CECIL GRAHAM. Well, you'll have lots of topics of conversation with *her*, Tuppy. (*Rising and going to him.*)

LORD AUGUSTUS. You're getting annoying, dear boy; you're getting demmed annoying.

CECIL GRAHAM (*puts his hands on his shoulders*). Now, Tuppy, you've lost your figure and you've lost your character. Don't lose your temper; you have only got one.

LORD AUGUSTUS. My dear boy, if I wasn't the most good-natured man in London——

CECIL GRAHAM. We'd treat you with more respect, wouldn't we, Tuppy? (*Strolls away.*)

DUMBY. The youth of the present day are quite monstrous. They have absolutely no respect for dyed hair.

LORD AUGUSTUS *looks round angrily.*

CECIL GRAHAM. Mrs. Erlynne has a very great respect for dear Tuppy.

DUMBY. Then Mrs. Erlynne sets an admirable example to the rest of her sex. It is perfectly brutal the way most women nowadays behave to men who are not their husbands.

LORD WINDERMERE. Dumby, you are ridiculous, and Cecil, you let your tongue run away with you. You must leave Mrs. Erlynne alone. You don't really know anything about her, and you're always talking scandal against her.

CECIL GRAHAM (*coming towards him L.C.*). My dear Arthur, I never talk scandal. *I* only talk gossip.

LORD WINDERMERE. What is the difference between scandal and gossip?

CECIL GRAHAM. Oh! gossip is charming! History is merely gossip. But scandal is gossip made tedious by morality. Now, I never moralise. A man who moralises is usually a hypocrite, and a woman who moralises is invariably plain. There is nothing in the whole world so unbecoming to a woman as a Nonconformist conscience. And most women know it, I'm glad to say.

LORD AUGUSTUS. Just my sentiments, dear boy, just my sentiments.

CECIL GRAHAM. Sorry to hear it, Tuppy; whenever people agree with me, I always feel I must be wrong.

LORD AUGUSTUS. My dear boy, when I was your age——

CECIL GRAHAM. But you never were, Tuppy, and you never will be. (*Goes up C.*) I say, Darlington, let us have some cards. You'll play, Arthur, won't you?

LORD WINDERMERE. No, thanks, Cecil.

DUMBY (*with a sigh*). Good heavens! how marriage ruins a man! It's as demoralising as cigarettes, and far more expensive.

CECIL GRAHAM. You'll play, of course, Tuppy?

LORD AUGUSTUS (*pouring himself out a brandy and soda at table*). Can't dear boy. Promised Mrs. Erlynne never to play or drink again.

CECIL GRAHAM. Now, my dear Tuppy, don't be led astray into the paths of virtue. Reformed, you would be perfectly tedious. That is the worst of women. They always want one to be good. And if we are good, when they meet us, they don't love us at all. They like to find us quite irretrievably bad, and to leave us quite unattractively good.

LORD DARLINGTON (*rising from R. table, where he has been writing letters*). They always do find us bad!

DUMBY. I don't think we are bad. I think we are all good, except Tuppy.

LORD DARLINGTON. No, we are all in the gutter, but some of us are looking at the stars. (*Sits down at C. table.*)

DUMBY. We are all in the gutter, but some of us are looking at the stars? Upon my word, you are very romantic to-night, Darlington.

CECIL GRAHAM. Too romantic! You must be in love. Who is the girl?

LORD DARLINGTON. The woman I love is not free, or thinks she isn't. (*Glances instinctively at* LORD WINDERMERE *while he speaks.*)

CECIL GRAHAM. A married woman, then! Well, there's nothing in the world like the devotion of a married woman. It's a thing no married man knows anything about.

LORD DARLINGTON. Oh! she doesn't love me. She is a good woman. She is the only good woman I have ever met in my life.

CECIL GRAHAM. The only good woman you have ever met in your life?

LORD DARLINGTON. Yes.

CECIL GRAHAM (*lighting a cigarette*). Well, you are a lucky
fellow! Why, I have met hundreds of good women. I never
seem to meet any but good women. The world is perfectly
packed with good women. To know them is a middle-class
education.

LORD DARLINGTON. This woman has purity and innocence.
She has everything we men have lost.

CECIL GRAHAM. My dear fellow, what on earth should we
men do going about with purity and innocence? A carefully
thought-out buttonhole is much more effective.

DUMBY. She doesn't really love you then?

LORD DARLINGTON. No, she does not!

DUMBY. I congratulate you, my dear fellow. In this world
there are only two tragedies. One is not getting what one
wants, and the other is getting it. The last is much the
worst; the last is a real tragedy! But I am interested to hear
she does not love you. How long could you love a woman
who didn't love you, Cecil?

CECIL GRAHAM. A woman who didn't love me? Oh, all my life!

DUMBY. So could I. But it's so difficult to meet one.

LORD DARLINGTON. How can you be so conceited, Dumby?

DUMBY. I didn't say it as a matter of conceit. I said it as a
matter of regret. I have been wildly, madly adored. I am
sorry I have. It has been an immense nuisance. I should like
to be allowed a little time to myself now and then.

LORD AUGUSTUS (*looking round*). Time to educate yourself
I suppose.

DUMBY. No, time to forget all I have learned. That is much
more important, dear Tuppy.

LORD AUGUSTUS *moves uneasily in his chair.*

LORD DARLINGTON. What cynics you fellows are!

CECIL GRAHAM. What is a cynic? (*Sitting on the back of
the sofa.*)

LORD DARLINGTON. A man who knows the price of everything and the value of nothing.

CECIL GRAHAM. And a sentimentalist, my dear Darlington, is a man who sees an absurd value in everything, and doesn't know the market price of any single thing.

LORD DARLINGTON. You always amuse me, Cecil. You talk as if you were a man of experience.

CECIL GRAHAM. I am. (*Moves up to front of fireplace.*)

LORD DARLINGTON. You are far too young!

CECIL GRAHAM. That is a great error. Experience is a question of instinct about life. I have got it. Tuppy hasn't. Experience is the name Tuppy gives to his mistakes. That is all.

LORD AUGUSTUS *looks round indignantly.*

DUMBY. Experience is the name every one gives to their mistakes.

CECIL GRAHAM (*standing with his back to the fireplace*). One shouldn't commit any. (*Sees* LADY WINDERMERE'S *fan on sofa.*)

DUMBY. Life would be very dull without them.

CECIL GRAHAM. Of course you are quite faithful to this woman you are in love with, Darlington, to this good woman?

LORD DARLINGTON. Cecil, if one really loves a woman, all other women in the world become absolutely meaningless to one. Love changes one—*I* am changed.

CECIL GRAHAM. Dear me! How very interesting! Tuppy, I want to talk to you.

LORD AUGUSTUS *takes no notice.*

DUMBY. It's no use talking to Tuppy. You might just as well talk to a brick wall.

CECIL GRAHAM. But I like talking to a brick wall—-it's the only thing in the world that never contradicts me! Tuppy!

LORD AUGUSTUS. Well, what is it? What is it? (*Rising and going over to* CECIL GRAHAM.)

CECIL GRAHAM. Come over here. I want you particularly. (*Aside.*) Darlington has been moralising and talking about the purity of love, and that sort of thing, and he has got some woman in his rooms all the time.

LORD AUGUSTUS. No, really! really!

CECIL GRAHAM (*in a low voice*). Yes, here is her fan. (*Points to the fan.*)

LORD AUGUSTUS (*chuckling*). By Jove! By Jove!

LORD WINDERMERE (*up by door*). I am really off now, Lord Darlington. I am sorry you are leaving England so soon. Pray call on us when you come back! My wife and I will be charmed to see you!

LORD DARLINGTON (*up stage with* LORD WINDERMERE). I am afraid I shall be away for many years. Good-night!

CECIL GRAHAM. Arthur!

LORD WINDERMERE. What?

CECIL GRAHAM. I want to speak to you for a moment. No, do come!

LORD WINDERMERE (*putting on his coat*). I can't—I'm off!

CECIL GRAHAM. It is something very particular. It will interest you enormously.

LORD WINDERMERE (*smiling*). It is some of your nonsense, Cecil.

CECIL GRAHAM. It isn't! It isn't really.

LORD AUGUSTUS (*going to him*). My dear fellow, you mustn't go yet. I have a lot to talk to you about. And Cecil has something to show you.

LORD WINDERMERE (*walking over*). Well, what is it?

CECIL GRAHAM. Darlington has got a woman here in his rooms. Here is her fan. Amusing, isn't it?

A pause.

LORD WINDERMERE. Good God! (*Seizes the fan*—DUMBY *rises.*)

CECIL GRAHAM. What is the matter?

LORD WINDERMERE. Lord Darlington!

LORD DARLINGTON (*turning round*). Yes!

LORD WINDERMERE. What is my wife's fan doing here in your rooms? Hands off, Cecil. Don't touch me.

LORD DARLINGTON. Your wife's fan?

LORD WINDERMERE. Yes, here it is!

LORD DARLINGTON (*walking towards him*). I don't know!

LORD WINDERMERE. You must know. I demand an explanation. Don't hold me, you fool. (*To* CECIL GRAHAM.)

LORD DARLINGTON (*aside*). She is here after all!

LORD WINDERMERE. Speak, sir! Why is my wife's fan here? Answer me! By God! I'll search your rooms, and if my wife's here, I'll—— (*Moves.*)

LORD DARLINGTON. You shall not search my rooms. You have no right to do so. I forbid you!

LORD WINDERMERE. You scoundrel! I'll not leave your room till I have searched every corner of it! What moves behind that curtain? (*Rushes towards the curtain C.*)

MRS. ERLYNNE (*enters behind R.*). Lord Windermere!

LORD WINDERMERE. Mrs. Erlynne!

Every one starts and turns round. LADY WINDERMERE *slips out from behind the curtain and glides from the room L.*

MRS. ERLYNNE. I am afraid I took your wife's fan in mistake for my own, when I was leaving your house to-night. I am so sorry. (*Takes fan from him* LORD WINDERMERE *looks at her in contempt.* LORD DARLINGTON *in mingled astonishment and anger.* LORD AUGUSTUS *turns away. The other men smile at each other.*)

Curtain

Fourth Act

SCENE—*Same as in Act I.*

LADY WINDERMERE (*lying on sofa*). How can I tell him? I
can't tell him. It would kill me. I wonder what happened
after I escaped from that horrible room. Perhaps she told
them the true reason of her being there, and the real meaning
of that—fatal fan of mine. Oh, if he knows—how can I
look him in the face again? He would never forgive me.
(*Touches bell.*) How securely one thinks one lives—out of
reach of temptation, sin, folly. And then suddenly—Oh!
Life is terrible. It rules us, we do not rule it.

Enter ROSALIE *R.*

ROSALIE. Did your ladyship ring for me?

LADY WINDERMERE. Yes. Have you found out at what time
Lord Windermere came in last night?

ROSALIE. His lordship did not come in till five o'clock.

LADY WINDERMERE. Five o'clock. He knocked at my door
this morning, didn't he?

ROSALIE. Yes, my lady—at half-past nine. I told him your
ladyship was not awake yet.

LADY WINDERMERE. Did he say anything?

ROSALIE. Something about your ladyship's fan. I didn't quite
catch what his lordship said. Has the fan been lost, my lady?

I can't find it, and Parker says it was not left in any of the rooms. He has looked in all of them and on the terrace as well.

LADY WINDERMERE. It doesn't matter. Tell Parker not to trouble. That will do.

Exit ROSALIE.

LADY WINDERMERE (*rising*). She is sure to tell him. I can fancy a person doing a wonderful act of self-sacrifice, doing it spontaneously, recklessly, nobly—and afterwards finding out that it costs too much. Why should she hesitate between her ruin and mine? . . . How strange! I would have publicly disgraced her in my own house. She accepts public disgrace in the house of another to save me. . . . There is a bitter irony in things, a bitter irony in the way we talk of good and bad women. . . . Oh, what a lesson! and what a pity that in life we only get our lessons when they are of no use to us! For even if she doesn't tell, I must. Oh! the shame of it, the shame of it. To tell it is to live through it all again. Actions are the first tragedy in life, words are the second. Words are perhaps the worst. Words are merciless. . . . Oh! (*Starts as* LORD WINDERMERE *enters.*)

LORD WINDERMERE (*kisses her*). Margaret—how pale you look!

LADY WINDERMERE. I slept very badly.

LORD WINDERMERE (*sitting on sofa with her*). I am so sorry, I came in dreadfully late, and didn't like to wake you. You are crying, dear.

LADY WINDERMERE. Yes, I am crying, for I have something to tell you, Arthur.

LORD WINDERMERE. My dear child, you are not well. You've been doing too much. Let us go away to the country. You'll be all right at Selby. The season is almost over. There is no use staying on. Poor darling! We'll go away to-day, if you like. (*Rises.*) We can easily catch the 3.40. I'll send a wire to Fannen. (*Crosses and sits down at table to write a telegram.*)

LADY WINDERMERE. Yes; let us go away to-day. No; I can't go to-day, Arthur. There is some one I must see before I leave town—someone who has been kind to me.

LORD WINDERMERE (*rising and leaning over sofa*). Kind to you?

LADY WINDERMERE. Far more than that. (*Rises and goes to him.*) I will tell you, Arthur, but only love me, love me as you used to love me.

LORD WINDERMERE. Used to? You are not thinking of that wretched woman who came here last night? (*Coming round and sitting R. of her.*) You don't still imagine—no, you couldn't.

LADY WINDERMERE. I don't. I know now I was wrong and foolish.

LORD WINDERMERE. It was very good of you to receive her last night—but you are never to see her again.

LADY WINDERMERE. Why do you say that?

A pause.

LORD WINDERMERE (*holding her hand*). Margaret, I thought Mrs. Erlynne was a woman more sinned against than sinning, as the phrase goes. I thought she wanted to be good, to get back into a place that she had lost by a moment's folly, to lead again a decent life. I believed what she told me —I was mistaken in her. She is bad—as bad as a woman can be.

LADY WINDERMERE. Arthur, Arthur, don't talk so bitterly about any woman. I don't think now that people can be divided into the good and the bad as though they were two separate races or creations. What are called good women may have terrible things in them, mad moods of recklessness, assertion, jealousy, sin. Bad women, as they are termed, may have in them sorrow, repentance, pity, sacrifice. And I don't think Mrs. Erlynne a bad woman—I know she's not.

LORD WINDERMERE. My dear child, the woman's impossible. No matter what harm she tries to do us, you must never see her again. She is inadmissible anywhere.

LADY WINDERMERE. But I want to see her. I want her to come here.

LORD WINDERMERE. Never!

LADY WINDERMERE. She came here once as *your* guest. She must come now as *mine*. That is but fair.

LORD WINDERMERE. She should never have come here.

LADY WINDERMERE (*rising*). It is too late, Arthur, to say that now. (*Moves away*).

LORD WINDERMERE (*rising*). Margaret, if you knew where Mrs. Erlynne went last night, after she left this house, you would not sit in the same room with her. It was absolutely shameless, the whole thing.

LADY WINDERMERE. Arthur, I can't bear it any longer. I must tell you. Last night——

Enter PARKER *with a tray on which lie* LADY WINDER-MERE'S *fan and a card.*

PARKER. Mrs. Erlynne has called to return your ladyships' fan which she took away by mistake last night. Mrs. Erlynne has written a message on the card.

LADY WINDERMERE. Oh, ask Mrs. Erlynne to be kind enough to come up. (*Reads card.*) Say I shall be very glad to see her.

Exit PARKER.

She wants to see me, Arthur.

LORD WINDERMERE (*takes card and looks at it*). Margaret, I *beg* you not to. Let me see her first, at any rate. She's a very dangerous woman. She is the most dangerous woman I know. You don't realise what you're doing.

LADY WINDERMERE. It is right that I should see her.

LORD WINDERMERE. My child, you may be on the brink of a great sorrow. Don't go to meet it. It is absolutely necessary that I should see her before you do.

LADY WINDERMERE. Why should it be necessary?

Enter PARKER.

PARKER. Mrs. Erlynne.

Enter MRS. ERLYNNE.

Exit PARKER.

MRS. ERLYNNE. How do you do, Lady Windermere? (*To* LORD WINDERMERE.) How do you do? Do you know, Lady Windermere, I am so sorry about your fan. I can't imagine how I made such a silly mistake. Most stupid of me. And as I was driving in your direction, I thought I would take the opportunity of returning your property in person with many apologies for my carelessness, and of bidding you good-bye.

LADY WINDERMERE. Good-bye? (*Moves towards sofa with* MRS. ERLYNNE *and sits down beside her.*) Are you going away, then, Mrs. Erlynne?

MRS. ERLYNNE. Yes; I am going to live abroad again. The English climate doesn't suit me. My—heart is affected here, and that I don't like. I prefer living in the south. London is too full of fogs and—serious people, Lord Windermere. Whether the fogs produce the serious people or whether the serious people produce the fogs, I don't know, but the whole thing rather gets on my nerves, and so I'm leaving this afternoon by the Club Train.

LADY WINDERMERE. This afternoon? But I wanted so much to come and see you.

MRS. ERLYNNE. How kind of you! But I am afraid I have to go.

LADY WINDERMERE. Shall I never see you again, Mrs. Erlynne?

MRS. ERLYNNE. I am afraid not. Our lives lie too far apart. But there is a little thing I would like you to do for me. I want a photograph of you, Lady Windermere—would you give me one? You don't know how gratified I should be.

LADY WINDERMERE. Oh, with pleasure. There is one on that table. I'll show it to you. (*Goes across to the table.*)

LORD WINDERMERE (*coming up to* MRS. ERLYNNE *and speaking in a low voice*). It is monstrous your intruding yourself here after your conduct last night.

MRS. ERLYNNE (*with an amused smile*). My dear Windermere, manners before morals!

LADY WINDERMERE (*returning*). I'm afraid it is very flattering—I am not so pretty as that. (*Showing photograph.*)

MRS. ERLYNNE. You are much prettier. But haven't you got one of yourself with your little boy?

LADY WINDERMERE. I have. Would you prefer one of those?

MRS. ERLYNNE. Yes.

LADY WINDERMERE. I'll go and get it for you, if you'll excuse me for a moment. I have one upstairs.

MRS. ERLYNNE. So sorry, Lady Windermere, to give you so much trouble.

LADY WINDERMERE (*moves to door R.*). No trouble at all, Mrs. Erlynne.

MRS. ERLYNNE. Thanks so much.

   Exit LADY WINDERMERE *R.*

You seem rather our of temper this morning, Windermere.

Why should you be? Margaret and I get on charmingly together.

LORD WINDERMERE. I can't bear to see you with her. Besides, you have not told me the truth, Mrs. Erlynne.

MRS. ERLYNNE. I have not told *her* the truth, you mean.

LORD WINDERMERE (*standing C.*). I sometimes wish you had. I should have been spared then the misery, the anxiety, the annoyance of the last six months. But rather than my wife should know—that the mother whom she was taught to consider as dead, the mother whom she has mourned as dead, is living—a divorced woman, going about under an assumed name, a bad woman preying upon life, as I know you now to be—rather than that, I was ready to supply you with money to pay bill after bill, extravagance after extravagance, to risk what occurred yesterday, the first quarrel I have ever had with my wife. You don't understand what that means to me. How could you? But I tell you that the only bitter words that ever came from those sweet lips of hers were on your account, and I hate to see you next her. You sully the innocence that is in her. (*Moves L.C.*) And then I used to think that with all your faults you were frank and honest. You are not.

MRS. ERLYNNE. Why do you say that?

LORD WINDERMERE. You made me get you an invitation to my wife's ball.

MRS. ERLYNNE. For my daughter's ball—yes.

LORD WINDERMERE. You came, and within an hour of your leaving the house you are found in a man's rooms—you are disgraced before every one. (*Goes up stage C.*)

MRS. ERLYNNE. Yes.

LORD WINDERMERE (*turning round on her*). Therefore I have a right to look upon you as what you are—a worthless, vicious woman. I have the right to tell you never to enter this house, never to attempt to come near my wife——

MRS. ERLYNNE (*coldly*). My daughter, you mean.

LORD WINDERMERE. You have no right to claim her as your daughter. You left her, abandoned her when she was but a child in the cradle, abandoned her for your lover, who abandoned you in turn.

MRS. ERLYNNE (*rising*). Do you count that to his credit, Lord Windermere—or to mine?

LORD WINDERMERE. To his, now that I know you.

MRS. ERLYNNE. Take care—you had better be careful.

LORD WINDERMERE. Oh, I am not going to mince words for you. I know you thoroughly.

MRS. ERLYNNE (*looking steadily at him*). I question that.

LORD WINDERMERE. I *do* know you. For twenty years of your life you lived without your child, without a thought of your child. One day you read in the papers that she had married a rich man. You saw your hideous chance. You knew that to spare her the ignominy of learning that a woman like you was her mother, I would endure anything. You began your blackmailing.

MRS. ERLYNNE (*shrugging her shoulders*). Don't use ugly words, Windermere. They are vulgar. I saw my chance, it is true, and took it.

LORD WINDERMERE. Yes, you took it—and spoiled it all last night by being found out.

MRS. ERLYNNE (*with a strange smile*). You are quite right, I spoiled it all last night.

LORD WINDERMERE. And as for your blunder in taking my wife's fan from here and then leaving it about in Darlington's rooms, it is unpardonable. I can't bear the sight of it now. I shall never let my wife use it again. The thing is soiled for me. You should have kept it and not brought it back.

MRS. ERLYNNE. I think I *shall* keep it. (*Goes up.*) It's extremely pretty. (*Takes up fan.*) I shall ask Margaret to give it to me.

LORD WINDERMERE. I hope my wife will give it you.

MRS. ERLYNNE. Oh, I'm sure she will have no objection.

LORD WINDERMERE. I wish that at the same time she would give you a miniature she kisses every night before she prays —It's the miniature of a young innocent-looking girl with beautiful *dark* hair.

MRS. ERLYNNE. Ah, yes, I remember. How long ago that seems! (*Goes to sofa and sits down.*) It was done before I was married. Dark hair and an innocent expression were the fashion then, Windermere!

A pause.

LORD WINDERMERE. What do you mean by coming here this morning? What is your object? (*Crossing L.C. and sitting.*)

MRS. ERLYNNE (*with a note of irony in her voice*). To bid good-bye to my dear daughter, of course. LORD WINDERMERE *bites his under lip in anger,* MRS. ERLYNNE *looks at him, and her voice and manner become serious. In her accents as she talks there is a note of deep tragedy. For a moment she reveals herself.*) Oh, don't imagine I am going to have a pathetic scene with her, weep on her neck and tell her who I am, and all that kind of thing. I have no ambition to play the part of a mother. Only once in my life have I known a mother's feelings. That was last night. They were terrible— they made me suffer—they made me suffer too much. For twenty years, as you say, I have lived childless,—I want to live childless still. (*Hiding her feelings with a trivial laugh.*) Besides, my dear Windermere, how on earth could I pose as a mother with a grown-up daughter? Margaret is twenty-one, and I have never admitted that I am more than twenty-nine, or thirty at the most. Twenty-nine when there are pink shades, thirty when there are not. So you see what difficulties it would involve. No, as far as I am concerned, let your wife cherish the memory of this dead, stainless mother. Why should I interfere with her illusions? I find it hard enough to keep my own. I lost one illusion last night. I thought I had no heart. I find I have, and a heart doesn't suit me, Windermere. Somehow it doesn't go with modern dress. It makes one look old. (*Takes up hand-mirror from table and looks into it.*) And it spoils one's career at critical moments.

LORD WINDERMERE. You fill me with horror—with absolute horror.

MRS. ERLYNNE (*rising*). I suppose, Windermere, you would like me to retire into a convent, or become a hospital nurse, or something of that kind, as people do in silly modern novels. That is stupid of you, Arthur; in real life we don't do such things—not as long as we have any good looks left, at any rate. No—what consoles one nowadays is not repentance, but pleasure. Repentance is quite out of date. And besides, if a woman really repents, she has to go to a bad dressmaker, otherwise no one believes in her. And nothing in the world would induce me to do that. No; I am going to pass entirely out of your two lives. My coming into them has been a mistake—I discovered that last night.

LORD WINDERMERE. A fatal mistake.

MRS. ERLYNNE (*smiling*). Almost fatal.

LORD WINDERMERE. I am sorry now I did not tell my wife the whole thing at once.

MRS. ERLYNNE. I regret my bad actions. You regret your good ones—that is the difference between us.

LORD WINDERMERE. I don't trust you. I *will* tell my wife. It's better for her to know, and from me. It will cause her infinite pain—it will humiliate her terribly, but it's right that she should know.

MRS. ERLYNNE. You propose to tell her?

LORD WINDERMERE. I am going to tell her.

MRS. ERLYNNE (*going up to him*). If you do, I will make my
name so infamous that it will mar every moment of her life.
It will ruin her, and make her wretched. If you dare to tell
her, there is no depth of degradation I will not sink to, no
pit of shame I will not enter. You shall not tell her—I forbid
you.

LORD WINDERMERE. Why?

MRS. ERLYNNE (*after a pause*). If I said to you that I cared
for her, perhaps loved her even—you would sneer at me,
wouldn't you?

LORD WINDERMERE. I should feel it was not true. A mother's
love means devotion, unselfishness, sacrifice. What could
you know of such things?

MRS. ERLYNNE. You are right. What could I know of such
things? Don't let us talk any more about it—as for telling
my daughter who I am, that I do not allow. It is my secret,
it is not yours. If I make up my mind to tell her, and I think
I will, I shall tell her before I leave the house—if not, I
shall never tell her.

LORD WINDERMERE (*angrily*). Then let me beg of you to
leave our house at once. I will make your excuses to Margaret.

> *Enter* LADY WINDERMERE *R. She goes over to* MRS.
> ERLYNNE *with the photograph in her hand.* LORD WIN-
> DERMERE *moves to back of sofa, and anxiously watches*
> MRS. ERLYNNE *as the scene progresses.*

LADY WINDERMERE. I am so sorry, Mrs. Erlynne, to have
kept you waiting. I couldn't find the photograph any where.
At last I discovered it in my husband's dressing-room—he
had stolen it.

MRS. ERLYNNE (*takes the photograph from her and looks at it*).
I am not surprised—it is charming. (*Goes over to sofa with*
LADY WINDERMERE, *and sits down beside her. Looks again*

at the photograph.) And so that is your little boy! What is he called?

LADY WINDERMERE. Gerard, after my dear father.

MRS. ERLYNNE (*lying the photograph down*). Really?

LADY WINDERMERE. Yes. If it had been a girl, I would have called it after my mother. My mother had the same name as myself, Margaret.

MRS. ERLYNNE. My name is Margaret too.

LADY WINDERMERE. Indeed!

MRS. ERLYNNE. Yes. (*Pause.*) You are devoted to your mother's memory, Lady Windermere, your husband tells me.

LADY WINDERMERE. We all have ideals in life. At least we all should have. Mine is my mother.

MRS. ERLYNNE. Ideals are dangerous things. Realities are better. They wound, but they're better.

LADY WINDERMERE (*shaking her head*). If I lost my ideals, I should lose everything.

MRS. ERLYNNE. Everything?

LADY WINDERMERE. Yes.

Pause.

MRS. ERLYNNE. Did your father often speak to you of your mother?

LADY WINDERMERE. No, it gave him too much pain. He told me how my mother had died a few months after I was born. His eyes filled with tears as he spoke. Then he begged me never to mention her name to him again. It made him suffer even to hear it. My father—my father really died of a broken heart. His was the most ruined life I know.

MRS. ERLYNNE (*rising*). I am afraid I must go now, Lady Windermere.

LADY WINDERMERE (*rising*). Oh no, don't.

MRS. ERLYNNE. I think I had better. My carriage must have

come back by this time. I sent it to Lady Jedburgh's with a note.

LADY WINDERMERE. Arthur, would you mind seeing if Mrs. Erlynne's carriage has come back?

MRS. ERLYNNE. Pray don't trouble, Lord Windermere.

LADY WINDERMERE. Yes, Arthur, do go, please.

> LORD WINDERMERE *hesitates for a moment and looks at* MRS. ERLYNNE. *She remains quite impassive. He leaves the room.*

(*To* MRS. ERLYNNE.) Oh! What am I to say to you? You saved me last night? (*Goes towards her.*)

MRS. ERLYNNE. Hush—don't speak of it.

LADY WINDERMERE. I must speak of it. I can't let you think that I am going to accept this sacrifice. I am not. It is too great. I am going to tell my husband everything. It is my duty.

MRS. ERLYNNE. It is not your duty—at least you have duties to others besides him. You say you owe me something?

LADY WINDERMERE. I owe you everything.

MRS. ERLYNNE. Then pay your debt by silence. That is the only way in which it can be paid. Don't spoil the one good thing I have done in my life by telling it to any one. Promise me that what passed last night will remain a secret between us. You must not bring misery into your husband's life. Why spoil his love? You must not spoil it. Love is easily killed. Oh! how easily love is killed. Pledge me your word, Lady Windermere, that you will *never* tell him. I insist upon it.

LADY WINDERMERE (*with bowed head*). It is your will, not mine.

MRS. ERLYNNE. Yes, it is my will. And never forget your child—I like to think of you as a mother. I like you to think of yourself as one.

LADY WINDERMERE (*looking up*). I always will now. Only once in my life I have forgotten my own mother—that was last night. Oh, if I had remembered her I should not have been so foolish, so wicked.

MRS. ERLYNNE (*with a slight shudder*). Hush, last night is quite over.

Enter LORD WINDERMERE.

LORD WINDERMERE. Your carriage has not come back yet, Mrs. Erlynne.

MRS. ERLYNNE. It makes no matter. I'll take a hansom. There is nothing in the world so respectable as a good Shrewsbury and Talbot. And now, dear Lady Windermere, I am afraid it is really good-bye. (*Moves up C.*) Oh, I remember. You'll think me absurd, but do you know I've taken a great fancy to this fan that I was silly enough to run away with last night from your ball. Now, I wonder would you give it to me? Lord Windermere says you may. I know it is his present.

LADY WINDERMERE. Oh, certainly, if it will give you any pleasure. But it has my name on it. It has 'Margaret' on it.

MRS. ERLYNNE. But we have the same Christian name.

LADY WINDERMERE. Oh, I forgot. Of course, do have it. What a wonderful chance our names being the same!

MRS ERLYNNE. Quite wonderful. Thanks—it will always remind me of you. (*Shakes hands with her.*)

Enter PARKER.

PARKER. Lord Augustus Lorton. Mrs. Erlynne's carriage has come.

Enter LORD AUGUSTUS.

LORD AUGUSTUS. Good morning, dear boy. Good morning Lady Windermere. (*Sees* MRS. ERLYNNE.) Mrs. Erlynne!

MRS. ERLYNNE. How do you do, Lord Augustus? Are you quite well this morning?

LORD AUGUSTUS (*coldly*). Quite well, thank you, Mrs. Erlynne.

MRS. ERLYNNE. You don't look at all well, Lord Augustus. You stop up too late—it is so bad for you. You really should take more care of yourself. Good-bye, Lord Windermere. (*Goes towards door with a bow to* LORD AUGUSTUS. *Suddenly smiles and looks back at him.*) Lord Augustus! Won't you see me to my carriage? You might carry the fan.

LORD WINDERMERE. Allow me!

MRS. ERLYNNE. No; I want Lord Augustus. I have a special message for the dear Duchess. Won't you carry the fan, Lord Augustus?

LORD AUGUSTUS. If you really desire it, Mrs. Erlynne.

MRS. ERLYNNE (*laughing*). Of course I do. You'll carry it so gracefully. You would carry off anything gracefully, dear Lord Augustus.

When she reaches the door she looks back for a moment at LADY WINDERMERE. *Their eyes meet. Then she turns, and exit C. follows by* LORD AUGUSTUS.

LADY WINDERMERE. You will never speak against Mrs. Erlynne again, Arthur, will you?

LORD WINDERMERE (*gravely*). She is better than one thought her.

LADY WINDERMERE. She is better than I am.

LORD WINDERMERE (*smiling as he strokes her hair*). Child, you and she belong to different worlds. Into your world evil has never entered.

LADY WINDERMERE. Don't say that, Arthur. There is the same world for all of us, and good and evil, sin and innocence, go through it hand in hand. To shut one's eyes to half of life that one may live securely is as though one blinded oneself that one might walk with more safety in a land of pit and precipice.

LORD WINDERMERE (*moves down with her*). Darling, why do you say that?

LADY WINDERMERE (*sits on sofa*). Because, I, who had shut my eyes to life, came to the brink. And one who had separated us——

LORD WINDERMERE. We were never separated.

LADY WINDERMERE. We must never be again. O Arthur, don't love me less, and I will trust you more. I will trust you absolutely. Let us go to Selby. In the Rose Garden at Selby the roses are white and red.

Enter LORD AUGUSTUS *C.*

LORD AUGUSTUS. Arthur, she has explained everything!

> LADY WINDERMERE *looks horribly frightened at this.* LORD WINDERMERE *starts.* LORD AUGUSTUS *takes* WINDERMERE *by the arm and brings him to front of stage. He talks rapidly and in a low voice.* LADY WINDERMERE *stands watching them in terror.*

My dear fellow, she has explained every demmed thing. We all wronged her immensely. It was entirely for my sake she went to Darlington's rooms. Called first at the Club—fact is, wanted to put me out of suspense—and being told I had gone on—followed—naturally frightened when she heard a lot of us coming in—retired to another room—I assure you, most gratifying to me, the whole thing. We all behaved brutally to her. She is just the woman for me. Suits me down to the ground. All the conditions she makes are that we live entirely out of England. A very good thing too. Demmed clubs, demmed climate, demmed cooks, demmed everything. Sick of it all!

LADY WINDERMERE (*frightened*). Has Mrs. Erlynne——?

LORD AUGUSTUS (*advancing towards her with a low bow*). Yes, Lady Windermere—Mrs. Erlynne has done me the honour of accepting my hand.

LORD WINDERMERE. Well, you are certainly marrying a very clever woman!

LADY WINDERMERE (*taking her husband's hand*). Ah, you're marrying a very good woman!

Curtain

Notes

(These notes are intended to serve the needs of overseas students as well as those of English-born users)

Act I

1 *Morning-room* − a sitting-room used in the morning, rather than the more formal drawing-room which would be used in the evening.

1 *at home* − willing to receive visitors.

2 *Selby* − evidently the name of the Windermeres' country estate. Wilde often adopted the names of English towns or districts for use in his plays; Selby is a town in Yorkshire, a county in the north of England.

2 *of age* − having reached the age of twenty-one, the age at that time set by law as the start of adulthood, when a man became legally responsible for his own affairs.

2 *Foreign Office* − the government office responsible for international affairs; its headquarters were in the fashionable London area of Whitehall.

3 *so hard up* − short of money.

3 *pay . . . compliments* − Lord Darlington uses the two senses of the word 'pay': one pays a compliment (makes a flattering or favourable comment about someone) and pays a bill (gives money in return for services or goods bought).

3 *a whole heap of* − a large number of.

3 *optimism* − believing the best of people rather than the worst, assuming that life is good.

3 *the world* − here referring to the world or society inhabited by Lord Darlington, that of the rich and privileged in England, particularly London.

4 *the bores* − boring or dull people.

4 *extravagant* − exaggerated.

4 *a Puritan* − used to describe a rather narrow, restrictively moral and self-righteous individual, one likely to mistrust pleasure of any kind.

4 *allowed of* − accepted as proper.

4   *behind the age* − out of date, old-fashioned, not keeping up with the fashions or attitudes of her contemporaries.

4   *a speculation* − something in which one invests money or resources in the hope of making some kind of profit.

4   *a sacrament* − a religious ceremony, a thing of mysterious and sacred significance.

5   *I won't hear of* − I will not consider the possibility, or allow to happen.

5   *putting an imaginary instance* − suggesting an example which is not drawn from real life but is merely an idea.

5   *more than doubtful character* − not believed to be respectable or honourable.

5   *console herself* − relieve her unhappiness by finding a lover.

5   *vile* − worthless, dishonourable.

6   *very hard on* − treat with severity, be unfairly disapproving of.

6   *mercenary* − interested in money and social position rather than honour.

6   *what the world calls a fault* − an action (such as unfaithfulness in marriage) condemned by society but which, perhaps, is not in itself evil.

6   *hard and fast rules* − rules which are rigidly fixed and have no possibility of being adapted to fit special circumstances.

6   *Puritan* − (see note on p. 4).

6   *modern affectation of* − the contemporary way of behaving, adopting a manner not true to one's real character.

7   *behind my back* − when I am not present.

7   *ball . . . only a dance* − 'ball' suggests a formal event involving a large number of guests; 'dance' suggests the less formal gathering of friends. In both cases there would be dancing.

7   *A small and early* − a party for a few people, taking place early in the evening.

7   *very select* − only a limited number of carefully chosen people allowed to attend.

8   *I don't know what society is coming to* − I can't understand and certainly do not approve of the changes taking place in polite society, in the standards of behaviour and the range of people admitted.

8   *make a stand against* − condemn publicly or take action to prevent.

8   *scandal* − something which outrages society, or simply the general talk of such an event (for example, widespread talk and condemnation of the love affairs of the rich and famous).

8 *getting elbowed into the corner* − made to feel of little importance, having their rightful position in society rudely occupied by someone else.

8 *nag at* − constantly find fault with and reproach.

8 *all the honours . . . the odd trick* − the reference is to a card game such as bridge or whist; 'honours' are the high-scoring cards, generally the kings, queens, jacks and aces, which can win a point by beating the other cards played in a round. 'The odd trick' means just one or two winning points in an otherwise weak hand of cards.

8 *depraved* − corrupt, extremely immoral.

8 *trivial* − not serious, frivolous, not concerned with matters of importance and therefore not to be taken seriously.

9 *as a concession to my poor wits* − making allowances for my inability to understand.

9 *such a trial* − placing great strain on or testing severely the patience and good nature of his family.

9 *inadmissible into society* − could not be accepted by polite society as a person respectable enough to know or have any dealings with.

10 *has a past* − has committed a sin or an indiscretion in the past which she now seeks to hide or to disclaim.

10 *they all fit* − they all seem possible because consistent with her present behaviour and character.

10 *woman of that kind* − a woman not considered respectable, one believed to have behaved without discretion or morality and likely to do so again.

10 *not at home to any one* − not prepared to receive any other visitors.

10 *domestic creatures* − an insulting way of suggesting that the girls are of no importance and fit only for routine household responsibilities.

10 *plain* − unattractive although not especially ugly, not interesting to look at.

11 *fancy work* − decorative sewing, embroidery, crochet or tapestry.

11 *dreadful socialistic* − this conveys the Duchess's disapproval of what she considers society's move away from a class system based on privilege.

11 *taken a house in Curzon Street* − rented a house in a very fashionable part of London, near Piccadilly.

11 *talk scandal* − (see note on p. 8).

11 *Mayfair* − the fashionable and expensive district just north of

Piccadilly in London.

11 *the Park* — St James's Park, which runs into Green Park; these provide an area of grass, trees, formal walks and carriageways between Piccadilly, Buckingham Palace and Westminster.

11 *Homburg or Aix* — two fashionable resorts in Europe where the rich gathered to take advantage of the springs of mineral water considered good for the health.

11 *susceptible* — easily attracted by pretty women.

11 *high-principled* — behaving according to a noble set of ideals or standards of conduct.

12 *after all kinds of petticoats* — pursuing all kinds of women, of every social class, physical type and character.

12 *without a character* — without giving her a letter of recommendation for future employers.

12 *little aberration* — unimportant breaking of the usual rules of behaviour.

12 *take . . . too much to heart* — be too upset by, take too seriously.

12 *come back to you* — be loyal to you once more.

12 *don't make scenes* — don't show much emotion, don't cry or lose your temper.

12 *the wretches* — people without shame or consideration for others.

13 *taking such notice of* — considering worth being attentive towards.

13 *the imaginary instance* — (see note on p. 5).

13 *bank book* — a book containing details of one's financial affairs, of deposits to and withdrawals from the bank.

13 *scandal* — (see note on p. 8).

14 *starts* — gives a sudden movement displaying surprise or shock.

14 *bank book* — (see note on p. 13).

14 *Curzon Street* — the temporary home of Mrs. Erlynne (see note on p. 11).

14 *mad infatuation* — irrational and irresponsible passion for.

14 *squander* — spend wastefully.

14 *infamous* — having a bad reputation, wicked.

14 *jealous of* — concerned to protect or defend.

14 *Your honour is untouched* — your good name and moral well-being have not been damaged.

15 *squander* — (see note on p. 14).

15 *tainted in my memory* — cannot be recalled to mind without seeming spoilt.

15 *take a house* — (see note on p. 11).

15 *conducted herself* — behaved.

16 *well born* — came of a rich and respected family.

16 *had position* — had respect and influence in society.

16 *threw it away* — recklessly gave it up, deliberately but irresponsibly.

16 *an error of taste* — misjudged, not right according to the standards of their society.

16 *get back into society* — be accepted by polite society once more.

16 *to receive* — to accept her as a guest, a person worth knowing.

17 *to dress for dinner* — to change into more formal clothes for the main meal of the day, as was customary in society then.

17 *good women* — virtuous, but also with the idea of being self-righteous. The play was originally called *A Good Woman*. Wilde questions the implied standards: (see also p. 58).

18 *make chasm after chasm* — create one deep misunderstanding and mistrust after another.

18 *too lax* — too careless, neglecting what should be done.

18 *make an example* — take definite action against one offender so as to teach others how to behave.

19 *crosses my threshold* — steps through the door into my house.

19 *ruin us* — destroy our relationship as well as our position in society.

Act 2

20 *Drawing-room* — a reception room, or sitting-room, used to receive guests or to spend the evening in, generally one of the most elegant rooms in the house.

20 *revived cards* — reintroduced the printed cards on which (young) ladies wrote down the names of the gentlemen with whom they agreed to dance.

20 *such particularly younger sons* — young men of good family but with no prospect of inheriting title or fortune because of having elder brothers who would claim both.

20 *so fast* — lacking modesty and discretion.

21 *the season* — a period from May to July when fashionable society gathered in London and many balls and receptions were given. Young girls of about 18 would make their début into society and hope to find an eligible husband during the season.

21 *you are run after* — people seek your company.

21 *Capital place* — splendid place.

21 *exclusive* — selective, very difficult to enter.

21 *your value* — Wilde exploits the two senses of 'value', meaning someone's personal qualities, but also their financial assets, their income and possessions.

21 *kangaroos flying about* − see p.34.

22 *young country* − lacking an ancient civilisation, or only recently brought to the attention of people like the Duchess of Berwick.

22 *chatterbox* − a rather patronising way to describe someone very talkative.

23 *worn to a shadow* − thin and pale from weariness.

23 *Demmed* − corruption of 'damned', used for emphasis.

23 *Egad!* − corruption of 'By God!'

23 *didn't leave a rag on her* − were totally destructive in their judgments about her, discussed every aspect of her life and character and found fault with everything. Lord Augustus then chooses to use the expression literally and to imagine with some pleasure Mrs. Erlynne left completely unclothed.

23 *deuced* − used for emphasis, like 'demned'.

24 *beating about the bush* − taking time before coming to the real point of a conversation.

24 *confounded* − used in the same way as 'demned' (see note on p. 23).

24 *tired of that game* − no longer amused by a particular quality.

25 *dream of such a thing* − even think about the possibility.

26 *starts* − (see note on p. 14).

26 *Quite a picture* − pretty enough to be a painting.

27 *thinks like a Tory, and talks like a Radical* − his real opinions are very conservative and traditional but he argues as if he were in favour of extensive political reform.

27 *That woman* − 'That' is used partly for emphasis, but also to convey disapproval.

27 *dowager* − the widowed mother of a son who has inherited his father's title and estate.

28 *straw-coloured* − fair-haired and fair-skinned. 'Straw', however, has rather insulting overtones, suggesting coarseness.

28 *fancy* − imagine, picture.

29 *absolute brute* − a man without refinement or compassion.

29 *That woman!* − (see note on p. 27).

29 *goes in for being so proper* − chooses to behave in a very respectable manner.

29 *a perfect nuisance* − 'perfect' is used for emphasis, meaning 'complete'.

29 *dance attendance* − be constantly beside her trying to please her.

30 *tainted* — spoilt, as if diseased or corrupted.
30 *gave him all my life* — dedicated all my time and passion to him.
31 *the world* — that part of society which Lord Darlington and Lady Windermere belong to.
31 *bear his name* — share his family name, as his wife.
32 *the Park* — (see note on p. 11).
32 *this monstrous tie* — the marriage-bond which now seems unjust in his eyes.
32 *our souls touched* — our deepest natures, our hearts and minds, responded to each other.
33 *talking scandal* — (see note on p. 8).
33 *Homburg* — fashionable resort in Germany, known for its natural mineral springs.
34 *vulgar* — common, lacking the style and elegance associated with that society in which the Duchess lives.
34 *horrid kangaroos crawling about* — (see p. 21).
34 *end of the season* — (see note on p. 21).
34 *one of Nature's gentlemen* — a phrase generally used in praise of someone who seems to have been born with those qualities of courtesy and gentility which others have had to learn. Here the phrase is used to suggest that Mr. Hopper lacks polish and refinement.
35 *a fright in flannel* — a creature without prettiness or charm and dressed in garments made of sensible, warm cloth (in this case, baby clothes).
35 *sister-in-law* — married to the brother of.
36 *propose* — ask her to marry him.
36 *a handsome settlement* — the gift of a large sum of money.
36 *picturesque background . . . proper background* — on the first occasion the word means the setting for an event, its attractive surroundings; on the second occasion it refers to a woman's family and education as well as her present surroundings.
36 *£2000* — this then had about seven times its present purchasing power.
36 *third cousin . . . second husband . . . some distant relative of that kind* — the joke depends upon the different uses of the number: third cousins have a common ancestor three generations back, thus are only distantly related; a second husband is simply the second man a woman has married (after divorcing or being widowed from the first), so here the term 'distant' may mean that the relationship is no longer, or never has been, intimate.
37 *In modern life margin is everything* — Nowadays the distinction

between 'enough' and 'too little' is of vital importance.

37 *broken the bond of marriage* — acted in a way which destroyed the basis of their marriage.

37 *bondage* — slavery, imprisonment.

37 *starts* — (see note on p. 14).

38 *make her apologies* — apologise to others on her behalf.

39 *club* — it was customary for men in London polite society to belong to a men's club where they could meet their male friends, eat, perhaps gamble, drink and stay overnight on some occasions. It was considered important to belong to one of the more exclusive and fashionable clubs.

Act 3

40 *Tantalus frame* — a device in which decanters or bottles of wine and spirits could be on display yet locked up, so inaccessible.

40 *entrammelled* — caught, trapped, helplessly under the influence of.

40 *brutes* — (see note on p. 29).

40 *fawn* — display unquestioning adoration. The word is used insultingly.

41 *icy heart* — no ability to feel love or passion.

41 *put me in their power* — given them the ability to hurt or ruin me.

41 *fatal* — bringing disaster and ruin.

41 *the brink of ruin* — very close to shame and dishonour which will destroy her. This is also what is meant by the 'hideous precipice', a precipice being a steep cliff.

42 *serve as a blind* — be used to distract attention from, to conceal.

42 *relations* — dealings, relationship.

42 *scandal* — (see note on p. 8).

42 *outrage every law of the world* — behave in a way which breaks the rules of their society, rules concerning proper conduct, moral standards, honour.

42 *the world's tongue* — the gossip and the criticism of people in society.

42 *vile paper* — a newspaper mainly concerned with scandal and sensational stories.

42 *hideous placard* — the sheets of paper on which the day's more sensational headlines are written to attract buyers for the newspapers. 'Hideous' because speaking of her disgrace.

42 *life of degradation* — she would consider a life degrading in which she was forced to live as the wife of a man who she knew was the lover of another woman.

42 *infamous* — (see note on p. 14).

42 *simple* — foolishly trusting and easily deceived.

42 *restraining herself* — deliberately keeping her feelings suppressed.

43 *decoy* — trick, lure into a trap. A decoy is a trained animal or bird, or the man-made model of one, used by hunters to distract their quarry (target) from the real danger.

43 *the abyss* — a deep, dark hole in the ground, or bottomless pit, used here to describe the ruin she is likely to bring upon herself.

43 *device* — trick.

43 *take me in* — fool me, successfully deceive me.

44 *at the mercy of* — able to be hurt by, depending on the kindness of.

44 *infamy* — wickedness.

44 *on any pretext* — for no reason whatever, either true or false.

44 *hold I have* — power I have, or knowledge that gives me power.

45 *had a heart* — were capable of feeling compassion or love.

45 *Women like you* — in other words, women without honour or decency, concerned to use their charms only to gain money and power.

45 *You are bought and sold* — you, like a common prostitute, form relationships only for the wealth or privileges they can bring, not for love.

45 *may be in store* — may happen in the future.

45 *fall into the pit* — suffer disgrace and ruin. In ancient Greece, for example, criminals were thrown into a pit.

45 *creep in by hideous byways* — try to gain admittance to society by disreputable, perhaps even dishonest, and undignified means; for example, by pretending to be what one is not, or by exploiting the weakness of others.

45 *an expiation* — a way of paying for one's sin and thereby being released from guilt.

45 *made a heart in one who had it not* — caused someone to experience love and compassion when previously they had been unfeeling.

45 *wrecked my own life* — destroyed my chances of happiness and success.

45 *the wit* — ability to think quickly and creatively.

46 *restrains herself* — (see note on p. 42).

46 *Save me!* — Save me from the disgrace and unhappiness that would result from my husband discovering me in another man's apartment late at night.

47 *slip out* — leave the room quietly, without being noticed.

47 *face them* — stay to meet them and try to convince them that all is well.

47 *lost* — Mrs. Erlynne's hopes of marrying Lord Augustus will be ruined if he discovers her in Lord Darlington's rooms so late at night.

47 *turning us out of the club* — they have been asked to leave their club (see note on p. 39).

47 *dream of* — even consider the possibility of.

47 *demmed* — (see note on p. 23).

48 *at the club* — (see note on p. 39).

49 *Wiesbaden affair* — evidently a scandal about some event in Mrs. Erlynne's past which was said to have happened in the German resort of Wiesbaden.

49 *Awfully commercial, women* — regrettably concerned with money before all other considerations.

49 *can raise the wind* — can afford to pay for the pleasures and dangers involved.

49 *a past before her* — the events of her past will continue to affect her future. This is an example of a paradox, a statement which contains two apparently contradictory ideas yet which makes sense.

49 *demmed* — (see note on p. 23).

49 *lost your figure* — become fat.

49 *lost your character* — become decadent, immoral; lost your virtue and your good name.

49 *lose your temper* — become angry.

49 *strolls* — walks casually, in a relaxed manner.

49 *no respect for dyed hair* — do not treat with respect people whose hair has gone grey or white and who have therefore dyed it to make themselves appear more youthful. Wilde has adapted the more usual phrase: 'no respect for these white hairs'.

50 *you let your tongue run away with you* — allow the pleasure you have in talking to lead you into saying things that you do not mean or are not true.

50 *talk scandal* — (see note on p. 8).

50 *gossip* — idle but not necessarily harmful chatter among a small group of people about the lives of their acquaintances.

50 *moralise* — express opinions about good and evil or tell others how they should live their lives.

50 *plain* — unattractive to look at, in a rather dull way.

50 *Nonconformist conscience* — a mistrust of pleasure and a concern with sin, commonly associated with the more extreme Protestant

sects within the Christian church. It is here used as a criticism, as
'Puritan' was earlier (see note on p. 4).

50 *when I was your age . . . you never were* — Graham implies that,
no matter what his actual age, Lord Augustus was never at the stage
of maturity which Graham now is (a blend of youthfulness and
sophistication).

51 *play* — play cards, gamble.

51 *led astray* — taught to behave wrongly (not usually, as here, taught
to behave respectably).

51 *all in the gutter* — all without honour and virtue, not deserving
of respect.

51 *looking at the stars* — have our thoughts directed towards those
whose virtue and beauty place them beyond our reach but whom we
can admire.

51 *instinctively* — acting on an impulse, without thought.

51 *a good woman* — (see note on p. 17).

52 *middle-class* — Graham uses the term scornfully to describe that
level of society occupied by people who are neither aristocratic nor
wealthy enough to win a place in fashionable society (*his* society) but
who are morally conventional and make a comfortable amount of
money, either in the professions (lawyers, doctors, bankers, teachers,
etc.) or through trade.

52 *button-hole* — a flower worn in the lapel button-hole of a man's
jacket.

52 *cynic* — someone who disbelieves in honesty and goodness and
who tends to express his views in a disdainful or sneering fashion.

53 *a man of experience* — a man who has lived long enough to know
the ways of the world.

52 *instinct* — knowledge or impulses one is born with rather than
those one has acquired through education or experience.

53 *talk to a brick wall* — talk to something incapable of listening
intelligently.

54 *upstage* — at the back of the stage, away from the audience.

54 *I'm off* — I'm leaving.

55 *scoundrel* — man without honour or decency.

55 *starts* — (see note on p. 14).

55 *slips out* — (see note on p. 47).

Act 4

56 *fatal* — likely to bring ruin, to cause the destruction of her
happiness.

56 *look him in the face* — meet him without feeling unbearably ashamed.

56 *didn't quite catch* — did not hear clearly.

57 *not to trouble* — not to spend time doing something.

57 *costs too much* — will have too serious or unpleasant an effect on their life.

57 *a bitter irony* — an unpleasant and distressing pattern of events which contradicts one's expectations or previous beliefs; things are not what they seem.

57 *starts* — (see note on p. 14).

57 *Selby* — (see note on p. 2).

57 *The season* — (see note on p. 21).

57 *the 3.40* — a train leaving at 3.40 in the afternoon (15.40 hours).

58 *a wire to Fannen* — a telegram to Fannen, the butler or steward of their country house.

58 *that wretched woman* — (see note on p. 27).

58 *a woman more sinned against than sinning* — a woman who has been the victim of other people's mistakes rather than making mistakes of her own. It is an adaptation of 'I am a man more sinn'd against than sinning' from Shakespeare's play *King Lear.*

58 *a moment's folly* — a foolish decision taken very quickly.

58 *assertion* — forcing their views on other people.

59 *inadmissible anywhere* — she cannot be accepted by any part of polite society (see note on p. 9).

59 *at any rate* — grant this request at least, if nothing else.

60 *on the brink of* — very close to.

60 *in person* — to do something oneself rather than using a messenger or other means.

60 *heart is affected* — generally this phrase describes a medical condition, but here it means that Mrs. Erlynne's feelings have been too much troubled.

60 *the Club Train* — a train running from London to the South Coast, specially equipped with restaurant facilities and luxurious seating. The term 'Club' has recently been revived by some airlines to describe their more luxurious class of travel.

61 *out of temper* — bad-tempered, irritable.

62 *preying upon life* — living by destroying the lives or happiness of others.

62 *sully* — make dirty, corrupt.

63 *count that to his credit* — regard that as something to be praised.

63 *mince words* — find a less disagreeable way of saying something unpleasant.

63 *vulgar* — common, lacking refinement, crude.

64 *a miniature* — a very small portrait.

64 *your object* — your purpose.

64 *how on earth* — in what possible way.

64 *pose as* — adopt the appearance of, pretend to be.

64 *Twenty-nine when there are pink shades* — in a soft and flattering light she can pretend to be even younger, to be twenty-nine.

65 *cherish the memory* — derive pleasure from thinking lovingly of.

65 *had no heart* — (see note on p. 45).

65 *doesn't suit me* — does not make me happy, and does not make me appear more attractive.

65 *critical moments* — times when important decisions are made, points of crisis.

65 *out of date* — no longer fashionable.

65 *fatal* — (see note on p. 56).

65 *propose to* — intend to, plan to.

66 *infamous* — associated with scandal and dishonour, wicked.

66 *dressing-room* — in large, wealthy houses it was customary for bedrooms to have a small room to one side where one's clothes were kept and where one got dressed.

68 *impassive* — showing no emotion.

68 *saved me last night* — (see note on p. 46).

68 *Pledge me your word* — promise me.

69 *a hansom* — a horse-drawn cab, forerunner of modern taxis.

69 *Shrewsbury and Talbot* — a company well known for making such horse-drawn cabs.

70 *carry off anything* — cope with any situation.

71 *came to the brink* — came very close to disaster and ruin.

71 *Selby* — (see note on p. 2).

71 *starts* — (see note on p. 14).

71 *demmed* — (see note on p. 23).

71 *at the Club* — (see note on p. 39).

71 *put me out of suspense* — no longer keep me anxiously awaiting her decision.

71 *gratifying* — pleasing and rewarding.

72 *accepting my hand* — agreeing to marry me.

72 *a very good woman* — (see note on p. 17).

Act 1. *Above:* Lord Darlington: 'I won't hear of it raining on your birthday' (p. 5) (1966). *Below:* Duchess of Berwick: 'Dear Lord Darlington, how thoroughly depraved you are!' (p. 8) (1945). *Right:* Duchess of Berwick: 'It was only Berwick's brutal and incessant threats of suicide that made me accept him at all' (p. 12) (1945).

Above: Act 1 — Lady Windermere: 'You should not mention this woman and me in the same breath' (p. 16) (1945). *Below:* Act II — Lady Windermere: 'Let me wait! My husband may return to me' (p. 32) (1966). *Right:* Act II — Lady Windermere: 'How alone I am in my life!' (p. 32) (1945).

Act II. *Above:* Mrs Erlynne (*seated, right*): 'I see that there are just as many fools in society as there used to be' (p. 35) (1945). *Below:* Lord Augustus: 'Dear lady, I am in such suspense!' (p. 39) (1966).

Act III. Lord Darlington's Rooms. *Above:* from the original production (1892). *Below:* from the 1945 revival.

Act III. Cecil Graham: 'Experience is a question of instinct about life.
I have got it' (p. 53) (1945).

Act III. Mrs. Erlynne: 'I'm afraid I took your wife's fan in mistake for my own' (p. 55) (1966).

Act IV. Lady Windermere: 'It's too late, Arthur, to say that now'
(p. 59) (1945).

Act IV. Lord Windermere: 'Margaret, if you knew where Mrs Erlynne went last night . . .' (p. 59) (1945).